WILLOW WORK

Mary Butcher

Mickle Print Ltd, Canterbury

For Alwyne Hawkins

First published 1986 by Dryad Press Ltd, London.
This edition published 1995 by Mary Butcher, Canterbury.
Reprinted January 1999

ISBN 0 9525541 0 0

Typeset and printed by Mickle Print Ltd
Westminster Road, Vauxhall Industrial Estate,
Canterbury, Kent CT1 1YY
Tel: (01227) 780001

Cover *shows a bolt of brown willow tied with the traditional twisted willow bind, a blackberry basket using brown and white rods alternately in the French rand to produce stripes, a square shopper and a herringbone weave waste-paper basket. A rapping iron, picking knife and bodkin are also shown.*

Contents

Acknowledgment

I would like first of all to thank Alwyne Hawkins who introduced me to willow as a weaving material and passed on his enthusiasm for it during his generous teaching.

I am also greatly indebted to Barbara Maynard whose tragic death robbed basketmakers of an extremely knowledgeable teacher. My thanks are also due to Nellie Pilcher, Fred Rogers and Ted Tween, all of whom have taught me much.

Fred Rogers gave me much valuable technical advice and Meg Tapley has read my manuscript and made most helpful suggestions. Sheila Virgo has helped by working through recipes. I have had many useful discussions with Olivia Elton Barratt and Kay Johnson. I would also like to thank Mick Duff of Lenham Heath for his photography.

It would not have been possible to write this book without the full support of my family. My mother-in-law, Hilda Butcher, typed the manuscript and cared for the children. My husband has given most valuable advice and comments and all have tolerated the willow in every corner of the house.

Since this book was first published in 1986, there have been many changes in the basketmaking world in this country. In addition to traditional practices has come an awareness of basketmaking using recycled material by a generation of craftspeople bringing a new invention and colour into baskets and a wide range of exhibitions. Strong links have been formed with European basketmakers, particularly in those Eastern European countries which have a strong willow tradition which parallels that in Britain.

At the same time, we have fewer fully apprenticed craftsmen working, people who know the full range of once common regional baskets with a specific purpose. I have spent much time recently meeting and working with these craftsmen, recording their techniques, learning their histories and finding out as much as I can about the scale of the industry in past times. Despite these changes however, I hope that the republication of this book in substantially its original form, will encourage new readers to make a few baskets for family and friends, or begin a life-long passion with willow.

Mary Butcher 1995

Introduction

The history of willow baskets in Britain goes back at least to the time of the lake villages at Meare and Glastonbury in Somerset, about 150 BC. Before the twentieth century willow was used extensively for baskets which had a very wide range of use. Woven material was used to support the walls of the medieval harbour at Dover, for carrying building materials and as part of the buildings themselves. Willow baskets were used for agriculture, as seed containers, gathering baskets and winnowing fans; for fishing; transport; and even war, where baskets filled with earth became protective ramparts and others were used to carry shells. A large number and variety of baskets was used in the home.

With the development of modern materials in the late nineteenth and twentieth centuries this widespread use of baskets has declined. Fruit and vegetables are sent to market in boxes or net bags rather than each in its traditional basket, and plastic has replaced many of the willow containers used domestically. However the recent revival of interest in rural crafts has increased our awareness of willow baskets. It is hardly possible these days to open a magazine without seeing interiors with baskets used to add warmth and interest as well as storage space. There is also a new appreciation of craftsmanship so that baskets are becoming valued for their beauty and the technical skills they represent.

Willow is one of Britain's traditional basket-making materials, being strong, light and durable. It retains its colour and develops a sheen with age and use. Baskets are made on the 'stake-and-strand' principle, the base being the strong foundation for the whole basket. More willow is pushed into this base and bent up to form a framework for the sides. Weaving of various patterns is used to hold the framework in position and strengthen the sides. At the top the willow of the framework is bent down and interwoven to form a strong rim or border. The shaping of the basket is a result of careful weaving and a good eye.

This book is intended to introduce the beginner to the basic techniques of basketmaking through a series of basket recipes. It starts with a simple basket. Each new recipe depends on the mastery of the basic techniques and also includes new processes so complete beginners should work through the book from start to finish. On reaching the end the worker will be able to make small baskets of all shapes and can then go on to larger work with heavier material.

Tools

Photo 1 Starting at the back: screw-block, commander, bodkins, side cutters; at the front from the left: weight, rapping iron, secateurs, penknife, shop knife, picking knife.

Relatively few tools are needed to make baskets and these are inexpensive. You may find you have something suitable in the tool box and will not need to buy anything.
A professional basketmaker would have the following tools:

1 *Bodkins:* These are strong tapering pointed metal tools with wooden handles. They vary from very fine, like a large tapestry needle, for miniature work to about 2.5cm (1in) at the thickest for heavy work and range from 5cm (2in) to about 25cm (10in) in length. Bodkins are needed for making gaps in the work as when finishing a border and inserting handles. Also the tight curves necessary for hasps and nooses are formed by wrapping rods round a thick bodkin.

For the work in this book a 21cm (8in) bodkin is ideal but a metal skewer or large metal knitting needle can be substituted.

2 *Knives:*

a) A *shop knife* has a good quality blade and an angled end. It is used for cutting willow and must be kept very sharp. A Stanley knife or good penknife can be used.

b) A *picking knife* has a wide curved blade that is sharpened all round the curve. It is used with a rocking and pressing movement for trimming ends inside and outside a finished basket. Its shape makes it possible to cut ends in awkward places. This tool was represented on the arms of the Company of Basketmakers when it was founded in 1569.

There is no real substitute for it but all ends can be trimmed off with:

3 *Pointed garden shears or secateurs:* These are used for cutting thick rods for base sticks or posts in square work and can also be used for picking off (trimming) baskets if they are sharp enough not to squash the willow.

4 *Side cutter:* These are like pliers with one flat side and are useful for fine work and close trimming of thin rods. They are really wire cutters and can often be bought cheaply in markets.

5 *Rapping iron:* This is a rectangular piece of iron, usually about 20-25cm (8-10in) long and 2-4cm (¾-1½in) wide with one edge thicker than the other. It is used for compressing the weaving so that there are no gaps. A hammer or any heavy object can be used instead but often the iron has a useful ring at one end which can be used as a commander.

6 *Commander:* This is a heavy metal rod with a ring at one end and a U-shaped piece at right angles at the other. Rods are pulled through and against the arms of the U to straighten them. The ring handle on the rapping iron can be used in the same way. For the work described here the rods can be straightened with the thumbs as most are not heavy.

7 *A measure:* This is essential for keeping a check on the size of the work. A stiff metre rule is ideal or a dowel rod can be marked out in centimetres with small nails. (This is what the blind use.)

8 *A plank:* This is a wooden board about 180 x 60cm (6 x 2ft) raised off the floor about 10cm (3-4in) and preferably with filled in sides.

9 *A lapboard:* This is a wooden board about 90 x 60cm (3ft x 2 ft) with one end raised about 10cm (3-4in) and preferably with filled in sides. The basketmaker sits on the plank or on a box if he is making something tall, with the board sitting across his stretched legs and sloping down away from him. The basket sits on the board tilting away from the maker. This helps control the shape. Most workers at home may prefer to sit at and place the work flat on a table. This is perfectly satisfactory.

10 *Weights:* These are used to hold the basket steady as it is being worked. Anything heavy can be placed in the basket, either large metal weights or stones.

11 *A large tank or trough:* This is used when soaking the willow in water and may be stone, galvanized iron or wood. It should be about 180 cm (6 ft) long and have a lip so blocks of wood can be wedged under it to hold the willow underwater. I use a pig trough but unless you are going in for basketmaking on a large scale the bath works very well!

12 *A grease horn:* This used to be a cow's horn full of tallow. A lubricant is sometimes needed on the bodkin to ease the entry of new willow into small spaces. Tallow is no longer easy to buy although plumbers merchants may have it, and soapy liquid or Vaseline are acceptable substitutes. Simply dipping the willow in water before pushing it in a space helps.

13 *A screw-block:* This is essential for making square baskets and the only substitute I can think of is a Workmate or perhaps a vice. It consists of two strips of wood each about 40-50cm (16-20in) long and 5-8cm (2-3in) wide and with long bolts and nuts, preferably butterfly nuts, through them both. The two pieces are separated, upright sticks are put between them and the wooden strips are tightened. This holds the sticks upright.

14 *Clothes pegs and string:* These are often useful, acting as a third hand!

15 *Hoops:* These are rings of willow or cane which can be made by bending a 6 ft rod round into a ring, tying a simple knot with the ends, and pulling them to adjust the size of the ring. The remaining ends are wrapped round the ring thus formed. The diameter of the hoop should be roughly equal to the diameter of the basket at the border.

After reading this you will see that it is possible to make baskets with only a knife or shears, a hammer, a ruler, a stone and somewhere to soak the willow. You may not need to buy anything before you start except the material itself.

The material and its preparation

Willow occurs in Britain in a great many forms but the one used for the baskets described here is *Salix triandra*, the almond-leaved willow. This is grown in Somerset as a commercial crop and produces strong fine rods with very little pith. It can be bought from a number of growers whose addresses are given at the end of the book. *Salix triandra* exists in many varieties with different coloured barks. Growers, particularly C B Hector & Son, are beginning to develop more of these now that there is an upturn in the fortunes of the industry. In East Anglia, Lancashire and the Trent area other species, *Salix viminalis and Salix purpurea* are or have been grown but are not easy to obtain.

The willow is sold in bolts, which are bundles of rods all one length done up with either twisted rods or metal bands, each measuring 94cm (3ft 1in) around at 5cm (2in) above the base of the bolt. (See cover photograph.)

The willow can be bought in three forms:

1 *Brown willow* is cut, and dried with its bark on. This is usually a dark greyish-brown but varies with the variety. It is springy to work with and needs longer preparation than other forms, but looks beautiful and has a delicious smell.

2 *Buff-willow* is cut, bundled up and placed in huge brick tanks and boiled in its bark for several hours. Tannin from the bark acts as a dye and turns the rods the characteristic rusty colour called buff. The soggy bark is easily peeled off before the buffed rods are dried and made into bolts for sale.

3 *White willow* has had the bark removed without boiling. This is only possible for a short period in spring so part of each crop is left uncut until the rising sap loosens the bark. Peeling is labour-intensive, involving either pulling each rod through two metal spring prongs called a brake or using a mechanical brake. To spread the season of preparation, bundles of rods cut in autumn and winter are placed in about 15cm (6in) of water in pits until they produce leaves in spring. They can then be peeled easily and over a much longer season.

These white rods tend to become honey coloured with age. Because of the labour of peeling them they are more expensive than buff rods, which in turn are dearer than brown. However they are lovely used for small household articles and look good in combination with brown.

WHAT TO BUY

All these colours of willow can be bought in bolts of different length, called 'six foots', 'three foots' and so on. Different lengths are necessary for different parts of a basket: the framework for instance using longer heavier rods than the weaving. One grower, Nigel Hector, has started producing 'starter bolts' of mixed length for people who do not wish to buy a lot of willow but need a variety of sizes. Details are given with the addresses at the end of the book but you will need the following sizes of willow to complete the baskets in this book: six foots, five foots, four foots, and three foots. Buff willow is probably the easiest to work and at first brown is best used for weaving only so try three foot brown before going on to anything larger.

PREPARATION OF THE WILLOW

When the bolts arrive

It is very useful to sort out the bolts as soon as they arrive. It makes it easier to select materials before starting a basket and it will enable you to become familiar with the rods, their thickness and length and their variations.

Sort each bolt or part bolt into three separate bundles based on the thickness of the rods about 15 cm (6 in) up from the butts. You should have a fine, medium and thick bundle for each length of rod you have bought. Label them carefully.

Before starting a basket

The dry willow is brittle and will break when bent so it must be soaked in cold water and then wrapped in a damp cloth and left for several hours to 'mellow'.

Soaking times

Length	Buff and white willow	Brown
3 feet	½-1 hour	2 days
4	1-1½	3
5	1½-2	4
6	2-3	5

White willow may need rather longer soaking than buff.

If you are in a hurry try hot water and shorter soaking times.

MELLOWING

Buff and white willow should be mellowed for four or five hours or overnight by wrapping it in a damp cloth (old curtains are useful!) so that the inner parts of the rod become fully pliable. Brown willow must be mellowed overnight at least.

When wrapped the willow should be kept in a cool place if it is to stay in good condition.

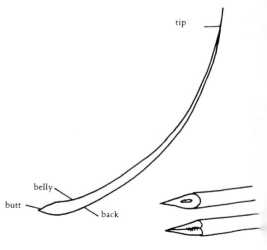

Fig 1 *A willow rod and two methods of slyping the butt*

Buff and white rods can remain wrapped for one or two days but must then be dried off. They can be resoaked for further use. If they remain wrapped or kept in a warm room they go greasy as moulds form and the rods will be soft and squash in use. Brown rods can be kept wrapped for a week or so before going out of condition.

If you find white rods split along their length in use it is likely they have been oversoaked or not sufficiently mellowed.

THE STRUCTURE OF A ROD (Fig. 1)

Each rod has a natural curve, the inside of this being the belly and the outside the back. The thick end is the butt and the thin end the tip.

Technical terms

Base sticks Short thick lengths of willow used as a foundation for the base. Usually the thickest willow used in a basket.

Bow mark Removal of the handle liners leaves a vertical space in the siding called the bow mark.

Chasing When slewing on an even number of stakes two sets of weavers are needed. One set passes in front of a stake, the other behind this stake. When weaving one set just catches the other up, chases it, but does not overtake it.

Cramming off The way stakes are trimmed and turned down at the border and pushed into the siding to finish off a plain rod border.

Cross handle A handle going from one side of the basket to another.

Crowning The shaping of a base so that it looks like an upside-down saucer and sits well on its rim.

Cutting out The sorting of willow rods before starting a basket to provide stuff for base weaving, stakes, siding, waling, etc.

Drafting Sorting a bundle of willow for length by holding it vertically and pulling out a handful of the longest, then the next, and so on. Useful when English randing.

English randing A stroke using one rod and carrying it in and out to its tip. The next rod starts on the right of the first. Butts are inside, tips outside. The sides of the basket are built up unevenly. One rod in each space between side stakes must be used if the basket is to be even.

False foot A ridge formed at the bottom rim of the basket. The stakes are carried under two to the right and brought up vertically for decoration.

Flow This refers to the angle of the sides to the base of the basket. If the stakes come out widely the basket has a pronounced flow.

French randing A weave for the siding using one rod in each space between stakes. With twenty four stakes twenty-four rods will be used. Gives a smooth side to the basket.

French slewing A weave used on the sides, like French randing but using two rods rather than one in each space between stakes. It therefore uses twice as many weavers as stakes in each round, and they must be fine. This weave is also called Double French Randing.

Handle bow A stout rod pushed into the siding in two places and forming the foundation of the handle. Normally bound or wrapped with much finer rods.

Handle liners Thick pieces of willow or sticks from the garden, slyped at one end and pushed into the upsetting to the left of a stake (viewing the basket from outside) to allow space in the siding for the handle bow.

Hasp The part of the fastening on a lid which passes over another loop to be fastened by a pin. Normally on the lid of a basket.

Herringbone weave A decorative variation of French slewing, using two sets of weavers, one being worked clockwise and the other anti-clockwise.

Hinge A movable joint attaching a lid to the body of the basket.

IM Inside measure

Noose The part of the fastening which is a loop on the side of the basket. The hasp fits over it.

OM Outside measure

Packing A way of building up one part of the siding by randing round only a few stakes, turning round one and working anticlockwise for a short distance and then turning again.

Pairing A weave using two rods, alternating them. Mostly used on bases.

Pegging Short pieces of dry willow are pushed into the handle bow between rows of waling. They prevent the handle being pulled out.

Picking off The method of cutting off all the unwanted willow ends with diagonal cuts using a picking knife or shears.

Plain rod borders The most commonly used border on willow baskets. It involves turning a number of stakes down behind one stake (three for a three rod plain border, four for a four rod, etc.) at the beginning. The border can be made wider by bringing these down behind two stakes instead.

Plait border A decorative border, of which there are several variations.

Pricking down The turning down of stakes before working the border. Done either against the thumb nail, the point of a knife as when pricking up, or by grasping the stake in the right fist and giving it a quick clockwise twist.

Pricking up The turning up of the stakes after staking up. A knife point is pushed into a stake and turned through a right angle while the rod is lifted with the other hand.

Randing A stroke used on square bases and lids, involving one weaver passing in and out between the stakes.

Reverse pairing A weave using two rods, alternating them and keeping them at the back of the work. Used to correct the twist on oval bases.

Rope border A simple border which gives the appearance of twisted rope.

Rope handle A handle which is wrapped with a spiral of finer rods.

Siding The weave used on the side of the basket.

Slath The arrangement of base sticks used to start the base.

Slath, tying in the The first few rows of pairing fix the slath in position.

Slewing A weave using two or more rods together as though they were one. An economical stroke as small tops can be used with little wastage and it is quick.

Slype A long diagonal cut made on the butt of the rod. Helps when staking up, putting in handle bows, etc.

Stakes The thickish rods used as the framework for the sides of the basket.

Staking up The process of putting the stakes into the base.

Stroke The different weaves used with willow are called strokes, i.e. pairing, randing, slewing, waling.

Trac border A simple border involving weaving pricked-down stakes in and out between the other stakes. A large number of variations are possible, many of which add extra height to the basket. Care must be taken to prick down stakes at the right height when starting so that the last stakes can be threaded into the spaces thus formed.

Twisted double rod small handle Small handle placed on or below the border. Formed from two rods, one of which forms a handle bow. Both are then twisted and used for wrapping the bow spirally.

Twisted single rod small handle A small handle used on borders, lids or halfway up the siding. Formed from one rod twisted along its whole length and used to give the effect of a three-strand rope.

Upsetting The weaving used after the stakes have been pricked up to hold them in position.

Wale or Waling A stroke using three or more weavers. Used for upsetting. Often used for strength.

1 Roundwork

A SMALL ROUND BASKET FOR FRUIT, BREAD ROLLS OR EGGS

This is a basic basket which uses many of the processes essential for a wide variety of baskets. It is very useful in the house. Looking round my kitchen I have one for eggs, one for clothes pegs, fruit in another and a jumble of nuts, bolts, elastic bands, and other bits and pieces in a fourth. I have used different coloured willows, and some are larger than others, but they all use the methods described below. It is good practice to make several, one after another (Photo 2).

Photo 2 The first basket. The central basket is directly from the recipe, the left-hand one has a larger base, a four rod behind two plain border (see p45) and the right-hand one has split willows (see p33) for the French randing. Both have double twisted rod handles (see p40).

Size

Outside height 10cm (4in), width at top 28cm (11in), measuring from the outsides of the border.

Materials needed

You will need three foot buff willows.
If your bolt is unsorted take about 1kg (2lb) of willow from the bolt and sort it into three bundles, thick, medium and fine.
If you have sorted your bolt on arrival take:
about fifty of the thickest rods for base sticks and stakes;
about twenty from the medium bundle for 'waling', a weave used at the start and finish of the side;
about fifty from the finest bundle for weaving the base and 'siding', weaving most of the side.

Tie the bundles up separately for soaking and mellowing and keep them covered with a damp cloth. (p10)
Your finished basket will not use all this material but soaking extra stuff allows you to select rods for various parts of the basket.
You will also need a willow hoop about 26cm (10in) in diameter.
HINT: Any willow unused when the basket is finished can be dried off and used again.

Photo 3 *The round base
showing the upper surface and edge*

The base (Photo 3)

This is the foundation for the rest of the basket. When I was taught I was told after my first lesson to go away and go on making bases until I could make them as well as my teacher - good advice! If the base is very uneven and poorly shaped it will be difficult to make a good basket with it. So if your first attempt does not quite resemble the photograph, do not get despondent but make another.

To start: making the slath

1   Take six of the thickest rods from the thick bundle and cut 22cm (8½in) lengths off the butts (thick ends) using secateurs or shears. These are called 'base sticks'.
2   Take one of these and split it for 7cm (2-3in) in the centre (Fig. 2a). A safe way of doing this is to hold the stick down firmly on a table or board, holding it with the thumb and first finger of the left hand, and push the tip of the knife firmly downwards into the centre of the stick using the right hand. Once the knife tip is through, pick up the stick with the knife still in it and twist the knife slightly to open the split.
HINT: Split at the side of the curve to help the crowning or curve of the base.

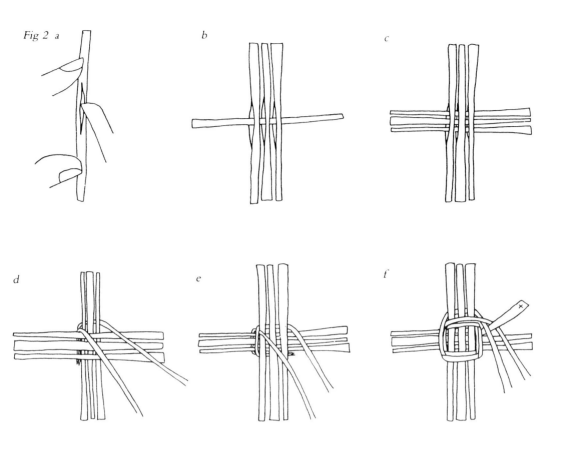

Fig 2 Starting the base:
(a) splitting a base stick
(b) threading on half the base sticks
(c) the finished framework for the base
(d) starting to weave with tips
(e) tying in the slath
(t) the finished slath and the start of pairing

3 Push one of the other sticks through the split. Now take two more sticks, split them in the same way and thread them on beside the first one (Fig. 2b).

HINT: *As you do this arrange the sticks so that the butts are alternating, not all on one side of the base. This makes it more even when finished, without one side being heavier than the other.*

4 Finally push the two unused sticks in through the three split ones beside the first, again alternating butt ends (Fig. 2c), You now have a cross of three sticks through three sticks. This cross or 'slath' of base sticks forms the strong framework for the whole basket and should be made with the thickest rods in the basket.

HINT: *This is so for all baskets, the only exceptions being with cross handles which have a thicker handle bow, and the stout corner posts in some square baskets.*

Starting to weave: tying in the slath

1 Select two fine long rods from your finest bundle of rods matching them as far as possible. Trim off 1cm (½in) from the tips if they are damaged. Push them both into one of the splits in the base sticks. Leave one of these rods at the front and take the other behind three base sticks and then bring it forward (Fig. 2d).

2 Now take the left-hand of the two rods in front of three sticks, pass it to the back on top of the second rod and then behind three sticks and bring it back to the front. It has been taken clockwise (Fig. 2e).

3 Now turn the slath a quarter turn anti-clockwise. Take the new left-hand rod in front of three sticks, behind and back to the front. Work round using the left rod as before until you have been right round the slath twice. This will leave one rod at the front and one at the back completing two rounds. You have now tied in the slath (Fig. 2f)

HINT: Each time you carry a rod to the back it should be on top of the earlier one.

Continuing to weave
The weave used follows that for tying in the slath and is. called 'pairing'. While you are weaving, the base sticks must be separated and spread out like the spokes of a wheel.

1   To start pairing
Pull the left-hand base stick (x in Fig. 2f) to the left, and bring the back rod forwards into the space you have made. Push it well down towards the centre of the slath.

2   Now take the left-hand rod, pass it in front of one stick, take it to the back in the same space (it passes on top of the other rod), carry it behind the middle base stick and forward in a space created by pulling the right-hand base stick gently to the right. Again push down towards the centre of the base.

HINT: Do not pull the rod too hard as this can distort the positions of the base sticks.

3   Continue weaving in this way, turning the base anti-clockwise as you go. Each rod is taken from the left, in front of one stick through to the back, pulled well down at the back (held there if necessary with the left forefinger) and brought gently forward again in the next space to the right.

HINT: If you try to take the rod to the back, behind a stick and forward again all in one movement you may find that there is a gap between your rows of weaving. It is much easier to get close weaving if you pull well down at the back after the first half of the stroke.
The rods should be pulled down firmly away from you but gently towards you.

4   Continue with this weave until the two rods run out.

5   To join (Fig. 3)
Select two more matched weaving rods and join as in the diagram, making sure you join butts to butts for an even row of weaving. The

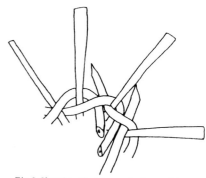

Fig 3 Showing the join used when pairing

new butts fit in to the right of the old ones, the new ones projecting about 3cm (1¼in) to the back (outside finished basket) and the old ones remain on the front (inside finished basket). All trimming of these ends is left until the base is finished.

HINT: Both rods should be joined at the same time to keep the weaving as even as possible.

6   Continue pairing as before but now adjust the positions of the base sticks to keep them as evenly spaced as possible. Just pull them gently into position before weaving round them. When this pair of rods runs out to the tips join in two more rods as before, this time joining tips to rips.
In pairing it is always 'butts to butts and tips to tips' when joining.

7   As you continue to weave push the base sticks slightly away from you to give the base a curve. This is called 'crowning'. A flat base will tend to sit on the slath and will wobble whereas a basket with a crowned base will sit on its rim and be much steadier and stronger. Weave until you reach the ends of the base sticks or as near them as possible, allowing for the fact that it is essential to end the base weaving with a pair of tips which taper gradually and produce a circular base. Ending with butts creates a gap in the finished basket and is ugly and weak.

When finished one tip can be threaded under the previous row of weaving to prevent any unravelling. Your finished base will be about 21cm (8in) across.

HINT: If your first base is not marvellous, do not be discouraged. Try another and be delighted by how much better the second one is. You will have got used to handling the material and be able to weave more evenly.

Picking off

All the ends on the base must be trimmed before continuing with the basket. You can use sharp shears or secateurs provided they do not squash the ends. Otherwise use a picking knife or penknife with a pushing and rocking motion, making a long diagonal cut. Make quite sure that the cut rod rests against a base stick and is not so short that it will slip through to the other side leaving a gap. Then the ends of the base sticks are cut off close to the weaving using shears.

HINT: This trimming is much easier to do if the willow is still damp so do not be tempted to leave the base for trimming later.

Staking up the basket (Photo 4)

This involves putting in the upright stakes which provide the framework for the sides of the basket. Twenty-four stakes are put in, one either side of each base stick.

Materials
From the pile of thickest rods select twenty-four which are evenly matched, particularly about 23cm (9in) up from the butts. This part of

*Photo 4 Two bases after staking up. The left-hand one has a hoop, held by bending one stake on opposite sides over it and twisting them round the hoop.
The right-hand one is tied with string.*

each rod will be used in the border of the basket and will be conspicuous so choose carefully. These twenty-four rods are called 'side stakes'.

To start

1 The butt ends of the side stakes must be 'slyped' (Fig. 1). A 'slype' is a 2cm (1in) long diagonal cut or pair of cuts made with a sharp knife to thin down the rod so it will fit into the base. One cut is made towards the butt, the rod is then rolled round a quarter turn, and the second cut is made. This leaves about half the rod uncut. Another method involves a single cut. The slypes should be made in the 'belly' of each rod, found by bending each gently to find its natural curve and cutting on the inside of the curve.

2 Now hold the base firmly in the left hand with the concave side towards you.Push a greased bodkin down beside one of the base sticks, to make a space, getting it as near to the centre as possible. Remove it. Take a slyped stake and push it firmly into the space with the cut surface towards you. Push it as far towards the centre of the base as possible (Fig. 4).

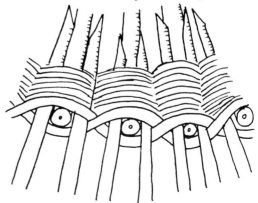

Fig 4 Showing stakes in position after staking up the base

3 Make another space with a bodkin the other side of the same base stick and push in a second stake as before. Continue until all the stakes have been put in, turning the base as you proceed.

4 Pricking up
This is a technique which allows very sharp bends to be made in rods.
Turn the base over so the convex side is uppermost.

Using the tip of the knife and with the base on a firm surface push it just into the stake about 3mm (⅛in) out from the base weaving. Then bring up the stake into a vertical position with the left hand while twisting the knife through a right angle (90°). Release the rod. It will fall back again but can now be bent up again in the same position without splitting (Fig. 5).

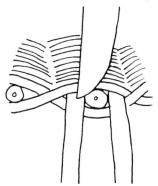

Fig 5 The position of the knife tip in the stake when pricking up

HINT: With small stuff such as the three foots used here it is possible to push your left thumb nail into the stake where the bend is needed and bring the rod up against that.

5 Holding up the stakes (Photo 4)

When all the stakes are in position they can either be gathered up above the basket and tied with string or held up with the hoop. This holds the stakes quite high up and, to stop it slipping off, the tip of one stake on each side can be bent down and wrapped round the hoop once or twice.

Upsetting

The stroke or weave used for this involves four rods, then three and is called 'waling'. It holds the stakes upright.

1   Take four matched rods as long as possible from the medium bundle. They should be less thick than the stakes. Sit with the concave surface of the base towards you and resting either on your knee or on a table.

2   Insert the four tips into a space in the base beside a stake (Fig. 6a) and now arrange the rods as follows. Take one rod behind one stake and bring it to the outside; another behind two stakes and to the outside; a third behind three stakes and out; and the fourth behind four stakes and to the outside. You now have the four rods coming towards you, each in its own space between two side stakes (Fig. 6b).

HINT: As you do this take care not to kink the rods. You may find it helps to curve each rod right round to the left before you pull it through. You will find your own method with practice.

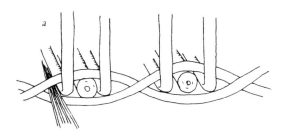

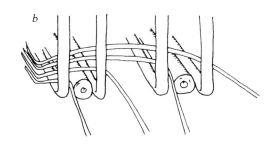

Fig 6 Starting the upsett:
(a) inserting the tips of four rods
(b) arranging them for the four rod wale

3   To weave the 'upsett'

Mark the stake to the left of the first rod with a clothes peg. Take the left-hand rod of the four, pass it across the front outside three side stakes, carry it to the inside, take it behind one stake and bring it out again. Tuck it well in next to the base weaving, pulling the stakes away from the base sticks to do it if necessary. Now take the new left-hand rod and take this in front of three stakes, behind one and back to the front. Pull it down towards you and leave it. Repeat this movement using each left-hand stake in turn until you reach the marked stake. This completes one round of upsetting or four rod waling (Fig. 7).

18

HINT: At every other stroke the rod can be tucked between the stake and the end of a base stick (Fig. 6b) to prevent any gap between the base and upsetting.

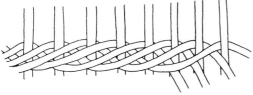

Fig 7 A four rod wale

4 *Changing to a three rod wale (Fig. 8)*

Before continuing with the second round of upsetting one rod is left behind, usually the one immediately to the left of the marked stake. It could be one of the others if one has been damaged.

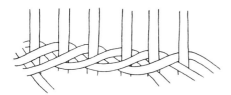

Fig 8 Changing from a four rod to a three rod wale

5 The weaving continues with each left-hand rod now passing in front of only **two** stakes and behind one.

6 Somewhere in this second round joins will have to be made (Fig. 9). Again here 'butts to butts and tips to tips' is the rule. The old butt is pulled to the left and another butt is pushed in beside it, with 3cm (1¼in) of the new end being left on the inside. All three rods must be joined in consecutive spaces. Join the left one first and weave with it, then the new left one and use it, then the third one.

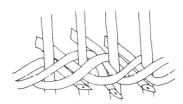

Fig 9 Joining in three new rods to continue waling

7 Continue weaving with the three new rods until the tips are reached. These tips are left on the outside and the upsetting is completed.

HINT: The first row of upsetting is almost on the bottom of the basket. If you have a gap between the edge of the base and the sides you should try to pull the upsetting rods further down towards you as you weave.

Siding

1 Take the hoop off now before starting to weave up the sides.

2 *French randing*

Before starting this weave put the basket on a table and put a heavy stone or weight inside to free your hands from holding it steady.

3 Select twenty-four rods from the finest bundle of stuff, making sure they are all about the same length. Then take one and put the butt end to the inside of the basket between two stakes and resting against the left-hand one. Using the left hand, hold this rod firmly on the outside against the next stake to the right with thumb in front, forefinger behind. With the right hand raise the rod slightly to kink it at this point and use the left thumb to push the rod to the inside, pass it smoothly behind one stake without kinking it and bring it back to the outside. Mark this rod by putting on a clothes peg about halfway along. Put in another rod in the same way in the space to the left of the first one used. Mark this with a second clothes peg (Fig. 10).

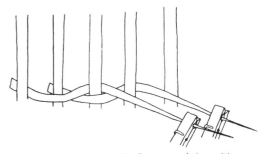

Fig10 French randing: the first two rods in position

4 Now continue putting in rods, making one stroke with each and leave them on the outside. The basket will have to be turned anticlockwise as you work as you always put in the next rod on the left of those already in position. Go round in this way until the two pegged rods are reached. There will now be two rods left of the original twenty-four.

5 Finishing the round

In order to complete the circle of weaving these two rods must be put in. These go in underneath the two pegged rods, one under each (Fig. 11). Each rod with a clothes peg will have to be pushed upwards to make it possible to put a weaving rod in underneath it. Put one in and weave one stroke with it. Then put in the second and weave it into position. Look at the inside of the basket and check that there is one rod for each side stake (one in each space) and that each has made one stroke. Make sure that all rods are sitting evenly at the end of the round before beginning the next round.

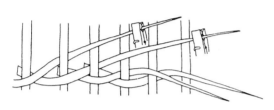

Fig 11 Finishing the round of French randing

6 The second round of weaving should be started with the right-hand of the two marked stakes, taking it in front of one stake, kinking it in the process, pushing it behind one with the left thumb and then bringing it back to the front (Fig. 12). Then use the second marked rod and continue as before. Again you will have to raise the two marked rods to complete the round.

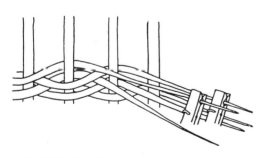

Fig 12 Starting the second round of French randing

HINT: *If you find two rods coming from one space it usually means that the lower one still has to do a stroke, so raise the top one before doing this to complete the round.*

Continue round in this way until you reach the tips of all the rods. Stop when the shortest rod has been completely used, taking care to finish with a complete round of weaving. Leave the tips on the outside. When more experienced there is no need to mark rods, and a new round can be started anywhere.

7 Rapping down

Take a rapping iron or small hammer and tap down on the rows of weaving to close them up and ensure that the top of the weaving is level. Parts that are raised can be hammered down a little more vigorously.

8 Top waling

To complete the weaving of the sides a few rows of waling must be put on to give a firm edge and visual definition.

1 A three rod wale is used, so select three matched rods from the medium bundle. Lay the tips to the inside of the basket in three consecutive spaces between stakes (Fig. 13). Take the left-hand rod in front of two stakes and behind one, leaving it on the outside. Then use the new left-hand rod in the same way and continue until the butts of the three rods are reached.

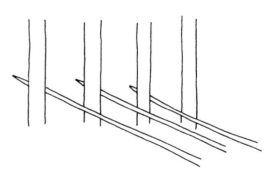

Fig 13 Starting the top waling with three tips

2 Join in three more butts of three more matched rods in the same way described under Upsetting. Weave as before until you reach the tips. This top waling should always finish with tips as they taper and give a smooth top to the basket.

3 Use the rapping iron to close down the weaving and make sure it is level and a regular height from the table top all the way round.

Stand a ruler on the table vertically and rotate your basket slowly next to it, rapping down any raised parts of the weaving.

HINT: A piece of dry willow cut to the outside height of the lowest part of the basket can be used instead of a ruler.

The three rod plain border

This finishes off the basket, giving a good edge which will stand up to wear. Plain borders are the most commonly used for willow baskets.

1 *Preparation*

Before starting work make sure the stakes are damp enough not to crack. If you have completed the siding fairly quickly they may just need a dip in water, but if the basket has been allowed to dry out it will need to be upended in a tub of water (I use a plastic dustbin!) and resoaked completely for the same length of time as the willow needed originally.

HINT: Stuff that is beginning to get too dry as you are working it tends to squeak. If your willow 'talks to you' dip it in water to redamp the surface. If you are working in a heated room you may need to do this frequently.

2 *Starting the border*

Bend down the stakes using a knife or thumb as when pricking up. This should be done about ½cm (⅛in) above the weaving.

HINT: It can look attractive if this bend is too high but not if too low.

Now bring a stake down behind the next on the right and leave it at the front. Repeat with the next two stakes to the right. These are the three rods from which the three rod border gets its name (Fig. 14).

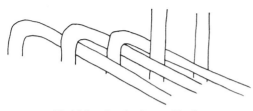

Fig 14 *Starting the three rod border*

3 Take the left-hand of these three and pass it in front of one upright stake, behind one and back to the front, moving it to the right all the time. Leave it with a loose curve (Fig. 15). Then bring the left-hand upright stake down beside it and on the inside of the basket (Fig. 16).

Fig 15 *The three rod border: take the left-hand stake in front of one, behind one, and back to the front*

4 Repeat twice with the new left-hand horizontal stakes, and bring two stakes down with them.

Now you will find the horizontal stakes in pairs. In subsequent strokes use the right hand, longer one of the pair leaving the lefthand one behind to be picked off later.

Fig 16 *The three rod border, bring one down beside it*

5 Continue these two movements until you reach the start again.

6 *Finishing the border*

You will have one stake still vertical (Fig.17a.1). The next horizontal stake to be worked (Fig. 17a.2) is taken in front of this and behind the next (Fig. 17a.4) which involves threading it through to the front as this stake has already been bent down at the start of the border.

HINT: To bend the willow without kinking it takes care. The willow can be made more malleable by stroking it with your right thumb on one side of the rod and your right forefinger on the other. Hold your thumb in a curve and run it firmly towards the tip of the rod. Repeat several times but if you do it too fast you will get friction burns!

When you come to thread the stake through (Fig. 17a.2) hold it in as wide a curve as possible and ease it slowly.

7 Take the remaining upright stake (Fig.17a.1), stroke it and thread it next to and behind the one just used (Fig. 17a.2).

You now have three pairs of stakes projecting towards you, all the rest being single (Fig.17b).

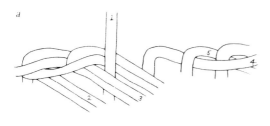

Fig 18 The first cram in position.
The positions of the other two crams are also shown

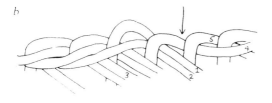

Fig 17 The end of the three rod border
(a) threading through at the end of the border
(b)The position of the first cram

8 *Cramming off*

Take the right-hand rod of the left-hand pair (Fig. 17b.3) and carry it to the right to sit in its final position alongside and outside the stake first bent down to start the border (Fig. 17b.4). With your knife or right thumb-nail prick down this rod, a few millimetres (⅛in) to the left of the second of the three stakes turned down at the beginning (Fig. 17b.5). Slype it about 4-5 cm (1½-2 in) below this point. Push a bodkin in as shown by the arrow (Fig. 17b) and push this slyped end into the space you have just made (Fig. 17c). Tap down the cram.

Repeat with the right-hand rod of the new left-hand pair, cramming it off to the left of the third turned-down stake (Fig. 18). Repeat with the right-hand rod of the remaining pair, cramming it beside the fourth rod to be turned down.

HINT: Always curve the first few rods used in a rod border so that the finished border does not narrow at this point.

Picking off

This is the final stage in making the basket. It involves trimming off the ends, either with good shears or a picking knife. Use diagonal cuts, making sure the ends are short enough not to be felt as you run your hand round the basket but long enough just to rest against an upright stake. If you cut them too short they may slip through leaving a gap in the work. Set aside all the stake tops for use in other baskets. Now stand back to examine and admire your basket.

A BLACKBERRY BASKET

This is another round basket. It uses the techniques of the first one but adds increased height and a 'rope' handle. I find it a very useful, though small basket, not only for gathering fruit and vegetables but for carrying a thermos and a few sandwiches in the car. My children use them for conkers in the autumn and you could also put a pot plant in one on the window-sill (Photo 5).

Size

Outside height 21cm (8¼ in), top diameter 27cm (10½in). (Outside measure OM)

Materials required

Three foot rods must be soaked and mellowed.
Either: use 1kg (2lb) mixed three foot rods
or: at least fifty rods from the thick bundle for base sticks and stakes, thirty from the medium bundle for waling and handle wrapping, and about sixty from the fine bundle for siding, and for base weaving.

You need a prepared willow rod, a little thicker than a pencil and at least 61 cm (2 ft) long for a handle bow. An ash or hazel branch from the hedgerow can be used if no suitable willow is available but should be curved and tied into shape before use. Trim off any buds.

Putting in handle liners

These leave space for the handle once the sides of the basket have been woven.

Take two pieces of willow, cane or stick from the garden about pencil thickness or a little thicker and slype one end of each. These are handle liners.

Push the slyped end into the upsetting immediately to the left of a stake (Fig. 19). Push the second one in on the other side of the basket exactly opposite the first, again on the left of a stake.

HINT: They do not need to be as tall as the finished basket as they can be pulled up before the siding swallows them. They will leave a space, called the 'bow mark', behind them. Take care not to weave above them.

ANOTHER HINT: If you forget to pull them up you can often push them out in small jerks by pushing a bodkin through the siding, into the handle liner, and pushing upwards.

Photo 5 A buff willow blackberry basket

The base

Use six base sticks 14cm (5½in) long cut from thick butt ends. Using two long fine rods tie in the slath and weave the base as before, making sure the weaving finishes with tips.

Staking up

Use twenty-four thick rods, slype and push in as before. This arrangement counteracts any curve the stakes may have and helps the shape of a straight-sided basket. Prick up. Put on a hoop a little smaller than the top size you want for your basket.

Upsetting

Again, use four matched rods less stout than the stakes and tuck in the tips (Fig. 6.) Complete one round of waling, drop one rod and continue with three as in the previous basket. Join in three more butts when necessary, and weave these three rods out to tips. Rap down all round to close up the weaving. Take off the hoop.

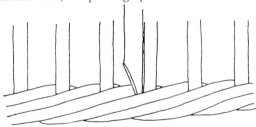

Fig 19 Putting in one of the handle liners

Siding

1 Use twenty-four matched rods to put in a band of French randing as in your first basket. Rap down the weaving to an even height all round.

As you weave you will have to control the stakes to give the shape you want to the basket. Use your left thumb and forefinger to place individual stakes as you weave round them, pulling them out if you want the basket to have flow or holding them up if you want it to be cylindrical.

HINT: The handle liners are treated as one with the stake they are next to. Both are woven round together. Pull the liners up now if necessary.

2 To increase the height of the basket select another twenty-four fine rods and work another complete band of French randing on top of the first. Rap down.

3 Variations (Photo 6)

You have a chance to add colour patterns to your next blackberry basket. The first band of French randing could be buff, the second white or vice versa. Alternatively two colours can be used when starting off the first band. Use buff willow to put in the first two rods and mark them with clothes pegs. Then put in two white weavers, then two buff and so on. This gives interesting spiral stripes round the basket. When you start the next band you will have to decide whether you want the stripes to continue those of the first band or whether you want a break in the pattern. Because of the outward flow of the basket the stripes in the upper half may be at a different angle from those below. Many other variations are possible e.g. three rods of one colour to one of another, remembering that the total number of rods in your rand is twenty-four. The total number of stakes in your pattern must divide into this number.

Photo 6 Three blackberry baskets.
On the left: brown band of French randing followed by a buff one. Handle liners still in position.
Central: a French rand using two buff rods then two white ones as the pattern. This gives a mottled effect. Handle bow in position.
On the right: the striped basket on the cover The bands of French randing are of alternate white and brown rods. This one shows a completed handle.

4 Top waling

As before start with the tips of three medium rods, work them out to butts, join in three butts and work the rods out to the tips.

HINT: Try to avoid the butts joining round the handle liners. They will then project when the handle bow is put in and may catch on clothing.

Rap down and level off the siding.

24

Border

Work a three rod plain border as before, leaving the handle liners above it (Photo 6 left). Work round them keeping the normal sequence of strokes.

Picking off

Trim the basket inside and out as before.

The rope handle

1 Pull out the handle liners.

2 Take the handle bow and slype the butt end with long 5cm (2in) cuts on the belly. Make use of the natural curve of the bow by arranging it so that its curve will help towards bending it to the opposite side of the basket and with the slype on the inside. Dip the bow in grease or water and push it into the bow mark on one side getting it as far in as possible, preferably as far as the upsetting.

3 Next judge how long you want the bow by bending it slowly and carefully over to the other side of the basket and judge how tall you want the finished handle. This is personal preference but in general low handles look better than tall ones and are stronger.

4 Slype the bow to give this height plus enough to push down to the upsetting. Again the cut surface will be on the inside. Grease it and push it into the remaining bow mark, getting it as far in as possible. Look at the height and adjust it now by pulling out this thinner end of the bow and slyping more off, if necessary (Photo 6 centre).

HINT: Pushing in the handle bow may be easier if you put the basket on the ground with several weights or stones inside (or your foot if the basket is bigger) and push down from above.

5 *Pegging*
Pegs are put in through the handle to stop the handle pulling out. Use a piece of dry willow less than ½cm (about ⅛in) wide and about 6cm (2¼in) long. Slype one end. Use a bodkin from the outside of the basket and, moving it from the right towards the left, push it between two rows of waling and pierce the handle bow (Fig. 20a). Take it out and push the slyped end of the dry piece in from the right and hammer it home through the bow. Pick off the ends with

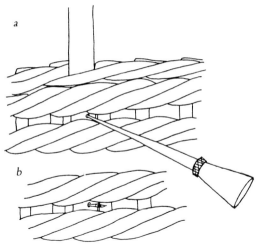

Fig 20 Pegging (a) pegging the handle bow (b) the peg in position

diagonal cuts so that they maintain the flat side of the basket but are just level with the outside of the basket (Fig. 20b).

6 *Starting the rope handle* (Photo 6 right) Select six three foots from the medium rods. Make sure they have no kinks or blemishes by bending each one in turn. Slype them at the butts. Take three and using a bodkin to make a space to the left of the bow where it enters the basket, push them in about 5cm (2in). Arrange them so that they cover the left and outside of the bow (Fig. 21).

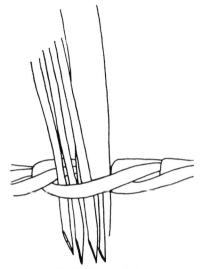

Fig 21 The handle bow with the first set of wrapping rods in position

7 Take them as a group and holding them in a very wide curve, carry them to the right, then under the handle bow and up on its left. They will have made one complete turn of the handle bow and be about 8-10cm (3-4in) up it (Fig. 22). Bring them round again in a repeat movement using them to spiral round the bow. Now they will lie at about the midpoint of the handle and will have made two complete turns in all. Make these movements slowly to allow the willow time to bend and avoid kinks. Make one more turn with them after which they should end up inside the basket a little above the border.

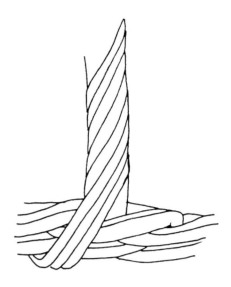

Fig 23 The inside view of the finished handle showing the wrapping rods going to the outside through the waling

there are large grins or gaps it will be necessary to use two more perfect three foots of medium thickness. Add one to each set of three roping rods and carry them round the handle as described.

10 *Finishing the handle*
To finish the handle dip the first set of four tips in water to redamp them and, take the two right-hand tips, twist them round each other a little and carry them in and out between the two rows of waling until they run out, leaving them on the inside where they can be picked off against a stake (Fig. 24). Carry the other two tips to the left, passing them over the outside of the bow and then in and out between the waling rows. Repeat with the four tips on the other side of the basket. Pick off any ends.

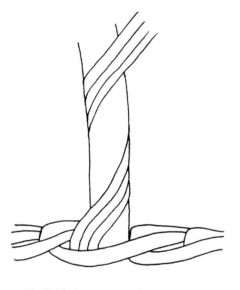

Fig 22 The first turn round the handle bow

8 Use a bodkin to make a gap between one row of waling and the next to the left of the bow when looking at the inside of the basket. Take one of the handle rods and gently push it to the outside through this gap. Carry it round in a large curve and ease it through. Repeat with the other three rods using them in sequence and when all the tips are on the outside pull them gently to make sure they are tight (Fig. 23). Leave them until later.

9 Now turn the basket round and push in the other three wrapping rods beside the other end of the handle bow and use them to rope the handle, filling in as far as possible the gap left by the first three. It is very difficult to get the handle perfectly covered as the outer length is greater than the inner length so try and space the wrapping rods as evenly as possible. If

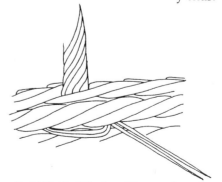

Fig 24 Finish off the tips of the wrapping rods by weaving them away

HINT: Why have a low handle? Any pull on a handle will come from putting heavy weights into the basket. If the handle is low this pull will tend to be at an angle to the sides of the basket. If it is tall it will tend to pull the handle vertically out of the siding and the handle will not be strong. Tall handles are suitable for decorative baskets or for flower arranging baskets but not for weight-carrying.

A ROUND SHOPPING BASKET

This is a strong basket with curved sides, much larger than the previous two and capable of carrying plenty of shopping. Longer, thicker willow must be used for the framework of base sticks and stakes (Photo 7).

Size

Base 21cm (8¼in) diameter
Height 21cm (8¼in), top diameter 37cm (14½in) (OM)

Materials

Five foots and three foots must be soaked and mellowed.

Photo 7 Round shopping basket

Either: use 1kg (2lb) of five foots for sticks, base weaving, stakes, waling and handle. ¼kg (½lb) of three foots for siding

or: select about forty five foots from the thickest bundle for sticks and stakes, forty from the medium bundle for waling and the handle, and sixteen or so fine ones for base weaving. Also prepare about seventy thick three foots for siding. You can use up the tops of stakes from the previous basket here.

You will also need a thick handle bow, about 2cm (¾in) across at the butt and a 36cm (14in) hoop.

The base

Cut six butts of thick five foots 22cm (8½in) long. Split three and thread three through as before. Use a pair of long fine five foots to tie in the slath and open up the sticks with pairing as before. Weave the base until about 21cm (8¼in) across, remembering to crown it well as this adds extra strength.

Staking up

Use twenty-four five foot rods a little thinner than the base sticks but from the thick bundle.

Slype them on the back to take advantage of their natural curve. Stake up so the slype will be downwards in the finished basket, using one each side of a base stick as before. Prick up and put on the hoop.

Upsetting

Use four five foots from the medium bundle, being not as heavy as the side stakes. Insert four tips and start waling, keeping the stakes outwards at an angle to the base. Do not let them come up to the vertical. If a good curved side is to be obtained it must start with the first rows of upsetting. After one round drop one rod, and continue with three, joining in three more butts as necessary and working these rods out to the tips.

Handle liners

Insert a pair of handle liners thicker than before and try to curve them a little to match the curve of the stakes.

Siding

1 Sort the tips into different lengths by holding a loose bundle of them upright and grasping a handful of the longest. Shake these loose and pull them from the bundle and put them on one side. Repeat three or four times. This is called 'drafing' the willow. Use the shortest tips low down where the basket has the smallest diameter. When you have used the drafts start using the three foots.

2 *Starting a two rod slew*
Take one rod and place the butt inside the basket, resting it behind one stake. Hold it firmly with the left hand against the next stake and use the left thumb to kink it to the inside, carry it behind a stake and bring it out again without kinking it further. Continue using this rod, taking it in and out, until you have used up half its length (Fig. 25).

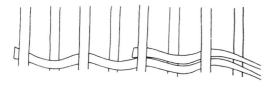

Fig 25 Starting a two rod slew

3 Now take a second rod and place it on top of the first, again with the butt on the inside of the basket against a stake. Take both rods together in and out between the stakes until the bottom rod runs out or gets too thin to be useful.

HINT: By this time you will be round the basket and a difficulty arises because of the even number of stakes in the basket. To overcome this difficulty you will need two sets of weavers.

4 *Chasing*
On reaching the beginning you will find one space between two stakes without any rods in. Start the second set here by putting in one rod, weaving with it for half its length and then putting in a second on top as before (Fig. 26). Continue weaving with this set until you just catch up but do not overtake the first set. Then complete a round with the first set.

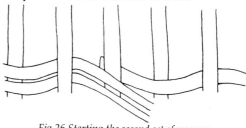

Fig 26 Starting the second set of weavers for a two rod slew

5 Continue weaving by putting in a new butt each time the bottom rod runs out so that you are always using two rods at a time. Do this with both sets of weavers.

6 Every few rows rap down on the siding to close down the weaving.

7 *Controlling the shape*
This is done by positioning the stakes with the left hand as you weave round them. If one is falling out slightly push it in as you weave round it and pull out those tending to go in. For this basket the first few centimetres of the weaving should be worked with the stakes angled out a long way. They are gradually brought in to the vertical and this gives the basket its curved shape.

8 Continue slewing until the basket is 18cm (7in) high (measured vertically from the table). Make sure the top is level, rapping down any places that are raised.

9 *Top waling*

Because this has a wider top than the previous basket waling is started in two places on opposite sides, to provide an even weight of weavers all round the top.

The tips of three five foot rods, thinner than the stakes, are laid into three consecutive spaces between the stakes. You can start anywhere. Use these to wale for half a round by taking the left-hand one, passing it in front of two stakes and behind one. Repeat with the new left-hand rod as described before.

Having worked halfway round lay in three more tips of five foots and work right round until you just catch up the first set. Resume working with the first set. Remember never to overtake a set.

After about one and a half rounds each set must be replaced by joining butts to butts (see first basket) and each new set worked out to tips.

Now level off the top of the basket with the rapping iron.

HINT: It helps if you can start the waling so that the butts do not finish in front of the handle liners. You can judge this by loosely holding the rods round the basket with the butts well away from the liners and see where you should start with the tips.

A four rod plain border

1 Prick down the stakes about 1cm (¼in) above the top waling.

2 Bring one stake down behind another as in the first basket, and repeat, this time with three more stakes. You now have four projecting towards you.

3 Proceed as in the three rod border (p21) by taking the left-hand one of these in front of one upright stake, behind the next and back to the front (Fig. 27). Bring the left-hand upright stake down beside it (Fig. 27 arrow).

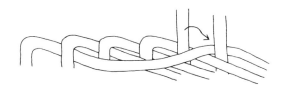

Fig 27 Starting the four rod behind one plain border

4 Repeat these two movements until you have been almost round the basket, always using the right-hand stake of the left-hand pair and bringing an upright stake to sit beside it.

5 When one upright stake remains take the right-hand of the left-hand pair, stroke it between your fingers and thumb and carry it in front of the upright stake and behind the next already turned down, threading it under this and to the front. Bring the upright down with it, again stroking and threading it. Now four horizontal ones remain to be used. These are crammed off in sequence as before.

Picking off

Trim the basket carefully inside and out.

The handle

1 Slype one end of the handle bow on its belly. Take out one of the handle liners and push in the bow after wetting or greasing it. Make use of any natural curve in the bow. Judge how tall you want the handle and cut it allowing enough to push into the siding. Slype on the inside of the curve and insert this end of the bow after removing the second liner.

2 Peg the handle as before.

3 Use four fine five foot rods, slype them and push them in on one side to the left of the handle bow as for the blackberry basket. Rope the handle, put in a second four on the opposite side and rope the other way. Finish the tips of these as before.

HINT: This very plain method of finishing handles is long lasting as there is nothing projecting at the border to receive wear.

Now you can go off shopping to try out your basket.

A SHALLOW BASKET WITH A PLAITED BORDER

This very delicate basket uses up a lot of the fine tops left from other baskets (Photo 8).

Size

Height 7½cm (3in), top diameter 29cm (11¼ in) (OM)

Materials

Prepare a large handful of tops, making sure that at least twenty-four of them are over

Photo 8 *A shallow basket with a plaited border*

46cm (18in) long for the stakes and at least thirteen long enough to complete at least one round of waling. These should all be about the same thickness at the butt.

You will also need six base sticks a little less than 1cm (¼in) diameter, and a 31cm (12in) hoop.

The base

Use six sticks 23cm (9in) long. Split three and thread the other three through. Tie in the slath with a pair of long tops and continue to weave with pairing, opening out the sticks as before. Pair until the base measures 23cm (9in) across, crowning it only very slightly and finishing the weaving with tips.

Staking up

Use twenty-four tops. Slype the butts on the belly and stake up as before with the slypes downwards. Prick up very close to the base as the waling rods are going to be very fine.

Put on a hoop 25cm (10in) across or tie the stakes with string.

Upsetting

Start with four tips, drop one after the first round, and join in butts to butts where needed. Continue the three rod wale to finish with tips. Take off the hoop or string.

Siding

1   Weave a two rod slew using short fine tops until the basket is 6.5cm (2½in) high on the outside.

2   *Top waling*

Start three rods with tips, work them round to butts, join in three more rods and work back to tips.

3   Level off the basket.

The border

This three rod plait gives a wide decorative border. Extra tops are used which are left in the border at the end to avoid a lot of threading through during which the rods may become kinked and ugly.

1 *To start the plait*

Select three fine rods which are the same thickness as the stakes remaining above the siding. Also find two short scraps of willow about the thickness of the butts of these. These are used as spacers to leave gaps that are helpful when finishing the border.

2 Put one of these in to the right of one stake at about 45° to the side of the basket (Fig. 28a). Bring the stake towards you over it, holding the stake also at 45° to the side but at right angles to the spacer.

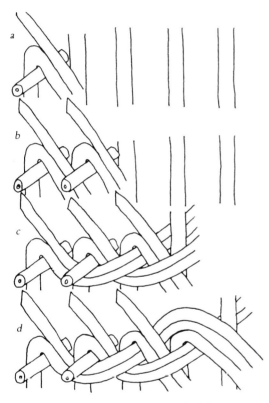

Fig 28 Starting the three pair plait

3 Put in the butt of an extra rod alongside and to the inside of this stake. Leave about 8cm (3in) of the butt projecting inside the basket (Fig. 28a).

4 Repeat steps 2 and 3 with the next stake to the right bringing it down over a spacer and putting in another spare rod, leaving 8cm (3in) of the butt inside the basket (Fig. 28b). You should have two pairs pointing towards you and to the right at an angle of 45° to the side of the basket.

5 Now take the left-hand pair, curve them in front of one upright stake and take them to the inside on top of the second pair. Make a wide curve and do not pull too tight (Fig. 28c).

6 Next bring the upright stake down (the curved pair acts as a spacer now) and add in the last extra rod as before. You now have one pair of rods on the inside and two on the outside, and three stakes have been brought down.

7 Weave as follows: the left-hand outside pair enter in front of one upright stake; the inside pair come out on top of them; the upright stake is brought down beside and on the outside of this pair (Fig. 28d).

8 Repeat these three movements. When you find you have three rods rather than pairs on the outside leave the inner one (the righthand one of the three) behind each time. Work round until you reach the start (Fig. 29a).

9 *To finish*

The two remaining pairs from the outside are taken to the inside. The left-hand pair takes the path of the first spacer and so passes under one pair (Fig. 29b). The other pair follows the second spacer, passing over one pair and under one pair (Fig. 29c). To prevent kinking these pairs stroke each rod first and move them through slowly. Leave them loose to match the rest of the plait.

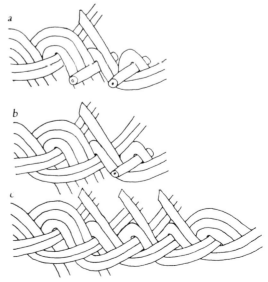

Fig 29 Finishing the three pair plait

10 Next deal with the three butt ends projecting to the inside. Each is tucked through to the front in turn after pulling aside each inside pair of rods to the left (Fig. 29d).

Fig 29d

11 Finally the right-hand rod of each of the three pairs remaining on the inside of the basket is taken through to the front and the left-hand one of each pair is picked off (Fig. 29e). The plait is now a complete ring, and

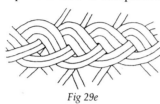

Fig 29e

there remains a continuous set of rods projecting to the outside and to the right all round the basket in addition to the three butt ends pointing to the left.

Now pick off the basket. The fine tips from the slewing can be saved for miniature baskets.

A SMALL ROUND BASKET WITH A ROPE BORDER

This pretty basket has a few unusual features which make it interesting. The rope border was not used commonly on English baskets but is found on European baskets and is very decorative (Photo 9).

Size
Height 14cm (5½in), top diameter 27cm (10½in).

Materials
Base: six 16cm (6¼in) pieces from five foots for the base sticks, and eight medium three foots for weaving it.
Stakes: forty-eight very fine three foots, carefully matched.
Waling: twelve three foots, not as fine as the stakes.
Weaving: at least twelve thick four foots.
A 25 cm (10in) hoop.

Photo 9 A rope bordered basket

Preparing the weavers

This basket is woven with split willows which give a slightly lighter look to the basket and a paler colour inside. To split the weavers take one of the thick four foots and cut the first 2cm (1in) or so of butt in half along the length of the rod. Then, tucking the tip under your left arm, put both forefingers into the split and both thumbs on the uncut surfaces of the rod. Pull the split ends apart gently and use the thumbs to provide pressure at the same time (Fig. 30). Gently slide your hands along towards the tip. If one side of the rod seems to be getting thicker than the other use more pressure from the thumb on the thick side. Work the split along as near to the tip as you can. Split all twelve weaving rods in this way.

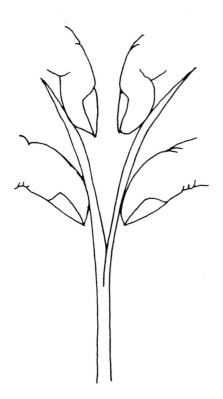

Fig 30 Splitting a willow rod by hand

The base

Make a slath of six 16cm (6¼in) lengths from the butts of five foots. Tie it in with three rounds of pairing using medium three foots, then open out as before and weave until eight rods have been used in the pairing.

Staking up

Use forty-eight fine three foots. Slype the butts on the belly and put in two on each side of each base stick (not one as before). Prick them up 5mm (⅛in) from the base and put on a 25cm (10in) diameter hoop.

Upsetting

Starting with four tips work one round of four rod wale, then change to three rod. Join in butts when necessary and work out to tips.
Take off the hoop if your stakes remain up-right.

Siding

1 Use the split weavers to put on a band of French randing, starting with the butts and with inner surface to the inside. Treat the pairs of side stakes as though they were one. Make the sides flow out so that its diameter is about 24cm (9½in) at the top. Finish the French rand with the ends on the inside at the top. It is easier to pick off these now to remove any lengths that may interfere with the border.

2 *Top waling*
Start with the tips of three foots. Use a three rod wale, join in three more rods and work back to tips.

The rope border

1 Slype two rods which match the stakes going into the border and insert one to the left of each of two consecutive stakes (Fig. 31a).

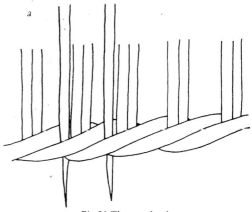

Fig 31 The rope border:
(a) putting in two rods before starting the rope border

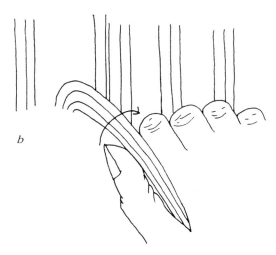

Fig 31b Twisting a group of stakes

2 Take the left-hand of these two groups and bring it horizontally towards you on the outside of the basket. Twist them clockwise by grasping them firmly and turning them towards the basket (Fig. 31b). Twist them up tightly and take them inside between the remaining group of three and the next vertical stake (Fig. 32a). Leave them loose with a gap under them.

3 Repeat with the next group of three and leave them to the inside between the next two pairs of vertical stakes. Again leave a space underneath (Fig. 32b).

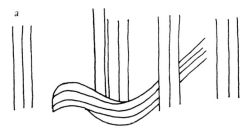

Fig 32 The rope border:
(a) the first twisted group in position
(b) the first two groups in position

4 Now bring the first group to the outside on the right of the first pair of vertical stakes and bring these forward with them. Twist them all towards the basket and curve them in between the next two pairs of vertical stakes. Treat the next group in the same way.

5 The border continues in this way but before using subsequent groups the two shortest rods are left on the inside when a group is brought to the outside for twisting. This keeps the twists the same thickness. Work round until you reach the beginning.

6 The last group are brought forward and twisted as before and are threaded through the small space left at the beginning (Fig. 33a).

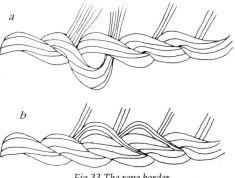

Fig 33 The rope border
(a) threading the final group to the inside
(b) building up the first two twists
by threading rods into them

7 You now have two groups remaining on the inside. Leaving two rods, bring the left-hand group outside and thread them away with the first three stakes used at the beginning of the border. Again leaving two rods inside bring the remaining group towards the outside and thread them away alongside the second group turned down for the border (Fig. 33b).
Now pick off the basket.

A ROPE-BORDERED BASKET WITH RAISED HANDLES

Proceed as for the previous basket until you are ready to work the border (Photo 10).

Size
Height at handle 16cm (6¼in). Diameter at top of handles 30cm (11¾in).

Photo 10 A rope bordered basket with raised handles

Planning the handles

The handles are left by working parts of the border well above the top waling. Each handle involves six pairs of stakes. Select these and mark them with a pen at the heights above the waling (Fig. 34). Make sure that they are not above the final tips of the top waling and that the handles are opposite each other.

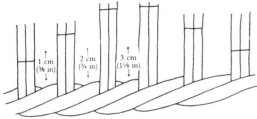

Fig 34 Markings for the handles on the rope bordered basket

The border

1   Start on the left-hand side of a flat section of the basket and work until you reach the marked stakes. This time instead of leaving two stakes behind on the inside as before bring them through with the rest of the group. If they are left on the inside, they interfere with the handles. Twist them all towards the basket and leave two behind on the outside before taking the rest on. Make sure you carry on with the two stakes you have just bent down. This will fatten up each 'twist' or rope.

2   When you reach the marked stakes prick them down on the marks and use them in the border in the usual way.
Pick off the basket, being particularly careful under the handles.

2 Oval work

A FIRST OVAL BASKET

Start with a small basket as it will be easier to control and only a little material has been used if it is not too successful. Most of the techniques are those used in the round baskets already described. There is one difficulty unique to oval work which must be overcome and that is the tendency of the base to twist. Once mastered the rest of the basket is straightforward (Photo 11)

Size
Base: 20cm (8in) long, 15cm (6in) across.
Height: 10cm (4in)
Width at top: 22cm (8¾in)
Length at top: 29cm (11½in)

Photo 11 The first oval basket.
On the left: white basket with brown siding
of the size given in the recipe
On the right: a buff basket
with brown siding and a greater flow

Materials
Use four foots, and three foots.
Either: soak about ½kg (1lb) of four foot stuff plus ¼kg (½lb) tops from previous baskets or very fine three foots
or: take about fifty rods from the thickest bundle of four foots, for sticks and stakes, twenty rods from the medium bundle for waling and about ¼kg (½lb) of the finest three foot rods or tops from previous baskets for weaving base and sides.

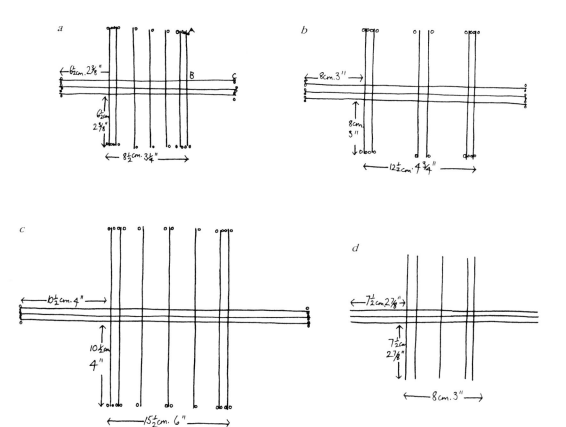

You will need an oval hoop about 26cm (10¼in) long, and about 21cm (8¼in) across. Tie a round one across to achieve the oval shape. Soak and mellow as before.

Fig 35 Plans of the four oval bases:
(a) the first base
(b) the shopper base
(c) the garden basket base
(d) the waste-paper basket base

The base

Unlike round ones, oval bases have two lengths of stick (Fig. 35a).

Cut three butts at 22cm (8¾in) (i.e. the length of the finished base plus 2 cm (1in) for ease of working), and seven butts 17cm (6¾in) for cross sticks.

Split the short sticks as before and thread the long sticks through. Arrange them as in Fig. 35a. At each end two short sticks are placed together. The outer ones in each case (Fig. 36) will be pulled round to help fill the half-circle at either end, and the inner one will remain straight. The remaining short sticks are equally spaced between these two outer pairs.

HINT: AB must equal BC for a regular base with half circular ends.

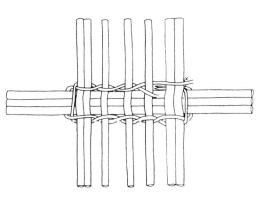

Fig 36 The base of the first oval basket showing the first round of pairing

Weaving the base

1   Select a pair of fine three foots and push the tips through the slit at x (Fig. 36) and bring one behind the group of three long sticks.

2   Bring the left-hand rod in front of this group, behind the next two sticks and back to the front.

3   Turn the base a quarter turn anticlockwise.

4   Now pair along the side of the basket, turn the base as you reach the other end and work round the groups of end sticks.

5   Weave round twice and then start separating the end sticks (Fig. 36) by bringing one rod up between two sticks.

6   Pull the sticks gently aside and pair between them as for a round base.

7   Join in the butts, arranging the join along one side of the base. This may mean leaving long butts from the first weavers but they can be trimmed later.

8   Continue pairing (Fig. 37a), gradually spreading the end sticks round the half-circles and keeping the side ones as straight as possible. Push the sticks slightly away from you to produce a crown on the base.

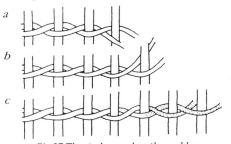

Fig 37 The strokes used on the oval base:
(a) pairing, with the rods at the front of the work
(b) taking the rods to the back to start reverse pairing
(c) pairing followed by reverse pairing

9   When you are about halfway out towards the edge you may notice that a twist has developed in the base. It can partly be overcome by gripping the base firmly in both hands and twisting it backwards and forwards a few times. But to correct it completely the stroke must be altered to pull the base in the opposite way and so counteract the pull of the pairing already done.

10   To start 'reverse pairing' take both weaving rods to the back (Fig. 37b). Now bring the left one up over the second, over the base stick and return it to the back. Repeat with the other weaver. Continue to weave, remembering to keep the rods at the back so that each stroke pulls down on the work (Fig. 37c). Continue until the base is the correct size, ending the weaving with tips.

Staking up

Select thirty-four matching four foot stakes and slype them on their bellies. Stake up using one stake on either side of all the sticks round the ends (Fig. 35, O = stake) but only on one side of the side sticks. The slyped surface will be downwards in the finished basket as before. It does not matter which side but space them as evenly as possible and keep the opposite sides even. Prick up the stakes and gather them into the hoop.

Upsetting

Use four four foots from the medium bundle and start with tips along one side of the basket. Complete one round of four rod wale, drop one rod as before, and continue with a three rod wale. Join in as necessary and work back to tips. As you work try to get a flow on the stakes at each end, by pulling them outwards. Take off the hoop.

Siding

1   Put on a band of French randing using thirty-four fine three foots, matching them as far as possible for length and thickness.

2   *The shape*
Shaping an oval basket needs care as the stakes have a horrible tendency to fall outwards at the sides but come inwards at the ends, often just what you do not want! The basket tries to become round. As you work use your left hand to hold the stakes where you want them as you weave round them. Pull the end ones well out as the weaving will tend to pull them in, but hold the side ones well in.

3   *Top waling*
Put on a three rod wale with three foots starting on one side, working halfway round and then starting again with a second set of three tips. Work the sets, chasing but not overtaking, and at the butts trying to keep the two sets of joins opposite each other.

4 Level off the work with the rapping iron.

The border
Work a four rod plain border (see p. 29).

Plaited end handles
These add decoration to the basket but can be left off.

1 First decide where the handles should go. Looking inside the basket trace the base sticks out to the stakes. Leave four stakes under the handle.

2 Select two fine three foots. Using a bodkin make a hole beside a turned-down stake to its left and push in one slyped butt (Fig. 38 right).

Fig 38 Small plaited handles
On the right: the start of the handle
On the left: finishing off the handle

3 Again using a bodkin insert the second rod under the border and under one row of waling perpendicular to the side of the basket. Pull it through to the halfway point and pull up both ends to the vertical beside the second rod.

4 Holding the two rods on the left and one on the right at an angle of about 60° to each other start plaiting by lifting the outside left-hand rod up and over its neighbour, taking it to the other side to lie on the inside of the right-hand rod.

5 Then use the outer right-hand one in reverse taking it up and over its neighbour to lie on the left of the inside rod. Continue these two movements, pulling the rods out to maintain the angle, until you have enough plait to curve over and make a handle which will allow you to hold the basket comfortably. You should be able to fit about three fingers under the highest part.

6 To finish (Fig. 38 left) slype the central rod and cram it off beside the border stake after using the bodkin to make a space. One tip is then taken over the edge of the border to the inside and passes under one row of waling to the outside. It is then woven in and out round the side of the basket to secure it. The other tip is taken over the border on the outside, passes in under one row of waling and is then woven away in the opposite direction.

HINT: You will find that slight differences in thickness of the rods make a great difference to the width of the handles, so choose your rods carefully.

Picking off
Trim away all the ends as before.

Alternative handles
Twisted willow handles could also be used on this basket although they are more difficult to do than the plaited ones.

Twisting a willow rod
This is a useful technique as it renders the willow rope-like. It will then travel round tight curves without any danger of kinking. Producing a good twist is a knack and will need practice. First pick a perfect rod and put it into the border of the basket so that it is securely held. The tip of the rod is then taken between the first finger and thumb of the right hand and rolled away from you to break up the rod. Then the left hand holds the willow rather loosely a few centimetres (inches) down. After the initial twist the tip is held firmly and the rod is moved clockwise as though you were moving the hands of a grandfather clock or were turning a handle. This movement involves the right wrist moving round in a circle and the circle will become larger as the twist moves down the rod. At the same time the left-hand first finger and thumb roll the rod away between them to assist the twist and gradually move down the rod, keeping pace with the twist. If the rod is a long one you can let go of the tip and move the right hand lower down. The tip will unravel but will twist up again easily later. If you want to twist only part of the rod the rod can be kinked to stop the twist moving further down. For these side handles take the twist right down to the border. If you find the willow splits into two or three sections along its length it probably means you

have not been cranking the tip round in large enough circles. Be bolder next time!

Twisted rod handles using two rods

1 First choose the positions for your handles. They should be as nearly opposite each other as possible and in this oval basket will be as wide as the gap between four side stakes.

2 Select two perfect matching rods about the weight of the stakes and slype them. Using a bodkin make spaces in the siding beside the two border stakes you have chosen. Insert the two rods, pushing them about 5cm (2in) into the siding.

The handle is worked on the far edge of the basket with your hands inside the basket and the bulk of the basket between you and the handle. It is not worked from the outside. The inserted rods will now be on the right of a side stake in each case.

3 The left-hand stake is bent over very gently after taking the 'spite' out of it by stroking with the right thumb in order to bend it and is taken to the outside of the basket and pushed from the outside to the inside on the right of the second handle rod and below the border and waling (Fig. 39a). A bodkin can be used to create this space before the movement is begun. This rod has now formed a handle bow and must bc adjusted slowly to give the willow time to take the curve without kinking, until at its maximum it is about two finger widths above the border. Try to make a handle which is horizontal rather than pointed in the middle.

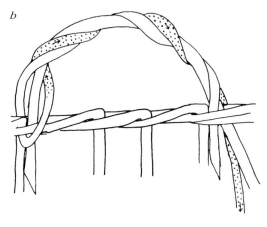

b

(b) the third stage

4 Twist up the second rod and take it round the handle bow to the outside and wrap it two and a half times round on its way to the left of the handle. It will reach this side on the outside of the basket and it is taken from the outside to the inside through the waling (Fig. 39a).

5 Take it back to the right again, passing it under the handle bow to start with and keeping it touching the twist that is already in position. Take it through on the right from the outside to the inside beside the handle bow rod (Fig. 39b).

6 Now drop this one. Take up the untwisted handle bow rod and twist it up. Carry it round the bow to the left of the first twist put in. It follows this round the bow and again passes from the outside to the inside on the left of the handle, again through the waling (Fig. 40a).

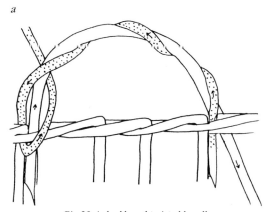

a

Fig 39 A double rod twisted handle:
(a) the first two stages

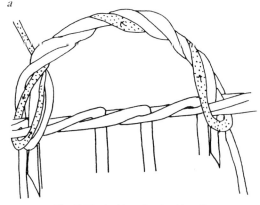

a

Fig 40 The double rod twisted handle:
(a) the fourth stage

b

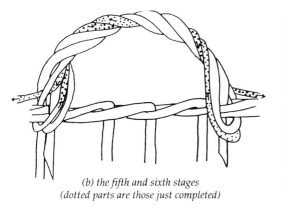

(b) the fifth and sixth stages
(dotted parts are those just completed)

7   Use it again to travel back to the other side, taking it under the bow to start with (Fig. 40b). On reaching the right-hand side of the handle it is pulled through between the handle bow and its neighbouring twisted rod. It is then cut off. It will be securely held, but it can be taken through the siding under the border and woven away.

8   Finally the twisted rod remaining inside the basket on the right travels to the left filling in the remaining gap (Fig. 40b). On reaching the left-hand side it is pulled through between the two twisted rods on the outside just before they go through the waling. If secure it can be cut off. Otherwise it can be woven away under the border.

In summary

Form a handle bow with the left-hand rod. Leave it on the inside. Twist the right-hand rod, take it round the bow, pass it from the outside to the inside through the waling and take it back to the right-hand side. Leave it. Twist the handle bow rod and take it to the left, through from the outside to the inside and back over the bow to the right. Anchor it and pick it off. Finally the remaining end is taken from right to left and anchored and picked off. The rods are all taken from the outside to the inside except just before they are dropped.

Picking off

Now trim the basket and tidy it up.
It may encourage you to know that even professional basketmakers may have to cut off their twisted rod handles and start again!

AN OVAL SHOPPER, MR HAWKINS' PATTERN

This is a plain strong shopping basket which should last many years. If properly picked off it will not snag your clothes (Photo 12).

Photo 12 An oval shopper
made by Alwyne Hawkins

Size

Height at handle 19cm (7½in) IM, top 46cm (18in) by 29cm (11½in).

Materials

Prepare about seventy five foots of white willow, if available, for stakes and waling. Otherwise use buff.

Also prepare some weaving material, about ½kg (1lb) or a large handful of three foots or tops. If you are going to use brown remember that it will have needed a few days to soak. Brown looks very attractive with the white.

You will also need nine fat butts of six foots for base sticks.

The base

Cut three fat butts 28cm (11in) long and six at 21cm (8¼in). Split the short ones in the centre as before and thread the long sticks through. Arrange the cross sticks as in Fig. 35b, keeping the two centre cross sticks together this time.

Weave the base with fine five foots working as before but keeping the two central short sticks together and working round them as if they were one.

Staking up

Slype thirty-two five foot stakes and insert so that the natural curve is used on the ends of the basket where flow is wanted. Slype on the back for this. Put in two stakes for each base stick, including one either side of the two central short sticks.

Put on the oval hoop from the previous basket.

Upsetting

In order to give a good ridge round the base and give a firm upsett the bottom waling is started with butts, four being inserted on each side so two sets of rods are used (Fig. 41). One set is worked round until the other set is reached. The second set is then used for a four rod wale until the first set is reached. One rod

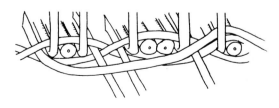

Fig 41 The oval shopper: starting the upsetting with butts

from each set is now dropped and a three rod wale is continued until the tips are reached. Take off the hoop.

Siding

1 When weaving, the two central side stakes are treated as one. Put in two 1cm (⅝in) wide handle liners between these two on each side.

2 Fine rods or tips of buff or brown are used for a two rod slew, starting off first one set and then another as before, as the basket has an even number of stakes. Shape the basket by pulling the stakes at the ends well out and trying to hold in the side stakes.

3 To counteract this flow at the ends and end up with a level top to the basket without too much rapping down it is necessary every third or fourth row to put in an extra slewing rod at each end. This produces a three rod slew and builds up the ends slightly. Avoid putting in these extra rods too far round the sides as the right-hand shoulders of each side would tend to become higher than the rest of the basket.

4 *Top waling*

Put in three tips on one of the left-hand shoulders of the basket and carry a three rod wale round to the point where three more rods are put in on the other left-hand shoulder. These two sets are woven out, more butts joined in and worked back to tips, as before.

5 Level off the basket.

The border

1 Before working the border one of each central pair of stakes is cut off immediately above the waling. Cut off the left-hand one on each side, looking from the outside of the basket.

2 A four rod plain border is worked.

3 Pick off the basket and remove the handle liners.

The rope handle

1 Find a handle bow about 1½cm (⅝in) wide, (a little wider than the handle liners) and insert it as before using the bow marks as a guide and remembering to get it down to the bottom of the slewing.

2 Peg this handle bow.

3 Rope as before but as it is a longer handle you will have to use four fine five foots on each side of the handle bow.

4 If you still have a gap all across the bow an extra rod can be slyped and put in on one side

and carried round to fill this. If there is not quite room for a rod spread those already used to make several very narrow gaps. These are less conspicuous.

5 Another method of finishing the handle

The four tips on the outside at one side of the handle are taken together up to the left of the handle, over the waling and border, round the inside of the handle and then to the outside again (Fig. 42). Here they cross over themselves, passing from top right to lower left and are taken through to the inside between the same two rows of waling they came through on the other side of the bow.

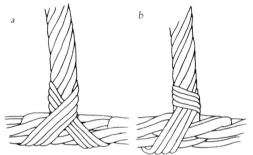

Fig 42 Finishing the handle of the oval shopper: (a) outside view (b) inside view

Now weave away these ends taking some one way and some another and passing them in and out between rows of waling and finally leaving them on the inside of the basket. Pick them off.

AN OVAL GARDEN BASKET

This is a stout basket used when weeding or for gathering vegetables as well as for cut flowers. It should last many years as willow does not rot at all easily even if kept damp for long periods (Photo 13).

Size
Height at handle 16cm (6¼in), top 56cm (22in) by 39 cm (15½in),

Materials
About fifty thick five foots for base sticks and stakes.
About thirty finer five foots for waling and roping the handle.
A large handful of three foots for the base and siding.
A stout handle bow at least pencil thickness.
An oval hoop of about 54 x 38cm (21 x 15in).

Photo 13 A garden basket

Photo 14 The garden basket showing the base

The base (Photo 14)

1 Cut out three thick sticks 38cm (15in) long and seven sticks 26cm (10in) long for the base sticks. Two sticks can be cut from one rod if it is thick enough.

2 Split the shorter sticks and thread the long ones through as before and arrange as in Fig. 35c, alternating the butts.

3 Use three foots for weaving and start pairing at one end by tucking in two tips. Pair round to the other end and tuck in two more tips which are then paired round to the first end.

4 Use the first pair again.

5 Continue until each part of the slath has been woven round three times and then start opening out the sticks at the ends as before.

6 Join in with butts when necessary, joining both sets of rods at the same time on opposite sides of the basket.

HINT: *Avoid joining at the ends because there is very little space.*

7 Keep twisting the base backwards and forwards to lessen the torque and when about halfway out change to reverse pairing.

8 Finish the base with tips.

Staking up

1 Select thirty-six five foots for stakes and slype them on the belly.

2 Stake up using a bodkin and tallow or water as before. Put in two stakes for each stick on the half circle, and two to each central side stick as in Fig. 35c.

3 Prick up about 1cm (¼in) from the base and gather the stakes into the hoop.

Upsetting

1 Start this with four tips of finer five foots on each side. Weave round, dropping one of the rods before weaving over the other set. Make sure the weavers are tucked well down between the stakes and sticks on the first round.

2 Join in three butts for each set and continue waling back to tips to finish the upsett. You will have used fourteen rods in all. After the first round use the waling to get an outward flow on the ends of the basket. Pull the stakes well out as you wale round them.

3 Take off the hoop and put in two stout handle liners between the two central stakes on each side. These two stakes are treated as one.

Siding

1 Using three foots put on a two rod slew, and keep the stakes flowing out only slightly at the sides and much more at the ends.

2 Keep examining the basket from above and sides to ensure both ends have the same flow. Keep the two central side stakes as one.

3 Slew until the basket measures 13cm (5in) from base to top of weaving at the handle position. The ends will be lower because of the outward flow of the basket and should not be specially built up this time.

4 Do not forget to rap down all the way round after each few rounds of weaving.

5 *Top waling*
Start with three tips of five foots on opposite sides of the basket as in the shopper.

6 Join in two sets of butts when the first rods run out and finish with tips.

7 Cut off the left-hand of the two central stakes (when looking from the outside) just above the top waling.

Border

1 Border down with a four rod behind two plain border. This is similar to the four rod plain border already described but is wider.

2 At the start the four rods are each brought down behind two stakes instead of one (Fig. 43a).

3 Then the left-hand one of these four is taken in front of two upright stakes (instead of one as previously), behind one and back to the front (Fig 43a). The left-hand upright stake is brought down beside it.

4 Continue like this until you are back to the start and have two stakes left upright.

5 Stroke the left-hand horizontal stake and thread it in front of these two upright stakes, and behind and under the next, threading it back to the front (Fig. 43b).

6 The left-hand upright stake is pricked down and threaded through beside it, passing behind the remaining upright on the way.

7 The last upright stake is pricked down, brought behind two stakes which have already been used in the border, and back to the front by threading it through (Fig, 43c).

8 The remaining five horizontal stakes are crammed off (Fig. 43c). Each passes in front of three pricked-down stakes and is crammed off to the left of the fourth.

9 Now pick off the basket.

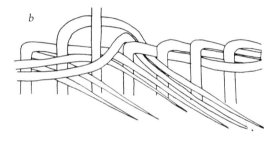

*Fig 43 The garden basket
with the four rod behind two plain border:
(a) starting the border
(b) threading the rods through
(c) threading the final upright stake
and putting in the first cram*

Handle

1 Take out the handle liners.

2 Slype one end of the handle bow and push it well down on one side.

3 Take the bow over to the other side of the basket to judge the handle height. About 28 cm (11 in) from the basket base to the highest point of the handle seems about right.

4 Cut off the bow level with the upsett on the far side, slype it and grease it and insert it. You may find you get more force for this if the basket is on the ground held down by one foot and you are pushing from above.

5 Peg the handle bow.

6 Rope the handle. Use four five foots each side and rope first one group round the handle and carry them through the waling as before.

7 Then repeat from the other side.

8 Weave away the tips as in the blackberry basket.

9 To increase strength and give a little decoration choose two more five foots. Slype the butt of one and push it in for about 5cm (2in) to the left of the handle bow with the outside of the basket towards you.

10 Push it firmly away from you to produce a right-angled bend and then use it to wrap tightly round and round the handle. Start the turns just above the border and work away from it, keeping the turns close together (Fig. 44a).

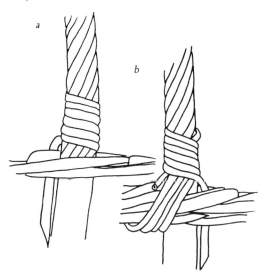

Fig 44 Finishing the handle of the garden basket. (a) outside view (b) inside view, showing the final position of the wrapping rod

11 When you have wrapped it round five or six times, push the tip vertically down under these wraps in a groove left by the handle wrapping rods. Pull the tip through and pull it tight (Fig. 44b).

12 Finally weave this tip away under the border to secure it.

13 Repeat on the other side of the basket.

AN OVAL WASTE-PAPER BASKET

This basket has a number of unusual features such as a method of staking up which is seen in Chinese baskets, and an attractive weave called French slewing, used on the sides. It is a very strong basket with a trac border (Photo 15).

Size
Height 29cm (11½in), top 27cm (10½in) by 23cm (9in).

Materials
Prepare a bundle of six foots, at least forty. The butts of eight thick ones will be used for base sticks, sixteen for side stakes and a further sixteen will be split and used for weaving the sides.
Also prepare about twenty-four five foots for base weaving and waling.

Photo 15 The waste-paper basket

The base

Use three butts from six foots 22cm (8½in) and five 18cm (7in) long. Split the short ones and thread the others through (Fig. 35d).

Using two thin five foots tie in the slath with three rows of pairing before opening out the sticks. Continue pairing until halfway out. Change to reverse pairing and work out to the stick ends, finishing with tips. Don't forget to crown the base. Cut off any protruding base sticks.

Staking up

Here only one stake is put in by each base stick. Use thick five foots or thin six foots, slype them on the belly and put in one on the left of each stick, working with the concave side of the base towards you.

The false foot

A decorative edge is created using the stakes. With the crown uppermost carry a stake to the right under two stakes and bend it up vertically on the right of a base stick (Fig. 45a). Hold it to the base with a clothes peg. Repeat with the next stake to the right and gradually work your way round.

The last two stakes will need to be threaded into position (Fig. 45b). The stakes all lean alarmingly to the right. Put on the hoop and try to pull them upright.

Upsetting

Start with three tips of thin five foots for a three rod wale (this is an exception to the rule of starting with one row of four rod wale). Work out to butts, join in three more butts and work back to tips.

Siding

1 Take the thirty-two split pieces (sixteen rods) of five foots and start as for French randing but use two split pieces side by side as though they were one (Fig. 46). Repeat in the space to the left. Mark these two pairs with pegs. Work round to the left putting two split pieces in each space and work one stroke with each exactly as for French randing. Complete the round by putting pairs in under the marked rods. Continue with rounds of French slewing, rapping down at intervals, until the basket is 25 cm (9¾in) high on the outside. Now take each pair to the inside and cut them off with shears, making sure they rest on a stake.

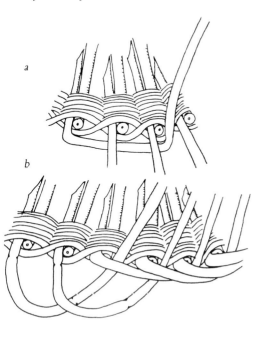

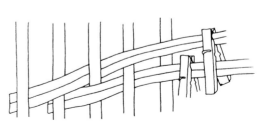

Fig 46 The waste-paper basket: starting the French slew

2 Top waling

Use six fine five foot rods, starting with three tips.

Trac border

A simple trac border complements the false foot at the bottom of the basket. It is not as strong as a rod border but will be strong enough for a waste-paper basket.

Start by pricking down one stake about the thickness of two stakes up from the top waling. Carry this stake in front of two stakes and to the inside (Fig. 47). Cut it leaving the end on

Fig 45 The oval waste-paper basket with the false foot.
(a) the start
(b) threading the last two through after kinking them
to help them lie correctly to complete the round

the inside against a stake. Repeat with the next stake to the right and work all round. The last two stakes must be threaded into position so that each space between stakes is occupied. Pick off the basket.

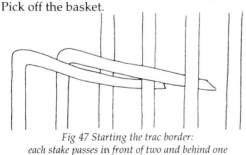

Fig 47 Starting the trac border:
each stake passes in front of two and behind one

A HERRINGBONE WEAVE WASTEPAPER BASKET

This weave produces a strong basket. It uses two sets of rods, the first moving anti-clockwise and the second clockwise, and is based on the French slew used in the previous basket (Photo 16).

Photo 16 The waste-paper basket using herringbone weave siding

Size

As for the previous basket.

Materials

As for the previous basket plus sixteen extra si foots, which must be split to give thirty-tw pieces.

The base, staking up and upsetting

As for the previous basket.

Siding

1 *The first round*
Put in the first round of French slewing exactl' as described in the previous basket.

2 *The second round*
Now take the extra thirty-two pieces and us them to start a band of French slewing in th opposite direction as follows. Take two spli pieces and put them in from above betwee two stakes with the butts on the right this tim (Fig. 48). Rest the butts behind a stake, the take the rods in front of the pair from the firs set and the stake to the left, over another pai from the left, behind the next stake and back t the front. They will project to the left.

Fig 48 Herringbone weave:
starting the second round of French slewing

3 The next pair is now used in the same way but to the right of the first pair. It is then taken in front of one stake, passing in front of the pair from the first row, behind one stake and out t the left.

4 Continue adding rods in this way to com plete the round, remembering that the first two pairs must be lifted so that the last two pairs can be put in, as when French randing.

Fig 49 Herringbone weave:
(a) raising the first set of weavers
before starting the third row
(b) raising the weavers for the fourth row

5 The third round

This will use the first set of rods again. You will find that they are below the second set of rods. To do a stroke put your hand down from above and hold a pair which project to the right just where they pass in front of a stake (Fig. 49a).

Pull them upwards and between two pairs of the previous row. This will carry them over the pair projecting to the left. Take them behind a stake to the right and back to the front.

6 Treat the next pair to the left in the same way. Continue working to the left until you have completed the round.

HINT: As you pull each pair upwards you must take care not to entangle them with the rods of the previous row, which may break.

7 The fourth round

This uses rods projecting to the left as did the second round. Lift a pair of rods just where it passes in front of a stake, cross it over a pair from the other set, then take it behind one stake and back to the front (Fig. 49b).

8 Now do the same with the pair to the right of the pair just used. Work round to the right with each pair in turn until the round is complete.

9 Repeat the third round instructions, then those for the fourth round and alternate these two rounds until the rods are getting thin or have almost run out. Rap down at intervals or the weaving will be loose.

10 Leave the ends on the inside by completing half a stroke with each pair so the ends rest inside a stake.
HINT: Often you have to stop weaving before completing the siding. When you start again begin with the lower weavers.

11 Complete the basket with the top waling and border as previously described for the French slewed waste-paper basket.

3 Square work

Photo 17 Front view of the square basket

All baskets with right-angled corners come under the title of square work, even if they are in fact long rectangles. They are the most difficult baskets to make. Start with a small rectangular box basket for sewing materials or letters. Leave larger picnic hampers until you have had a little experience!

A SMALL SQUARE LIDDED BASKET

This has a lid, blunt corners and hinges and a simple hasp and noose (Photo 17).

Size
Height without lid 17cm (6½in), top 29cm (11½in) by 22cm (8½in).

Materials
About eight thick six foots for edges of base and lid.
About twenty thick five foots for base and lid sticks, the tops of which will be used for hinges and fastenings.

Twenty-eight thick three foots for stakes.
A large handful of medium three foots for base and lid weaving, siding and waling.

The base

For this you need the screw-block (Fig. 50). The base sticks are arranged vertically in this, with the outer being heavier than the inner ones and usually with two at the outside edges for strength. Select straight sticks or straighten them carefully with the thumbs or the commander before you start. Use dry sticks as they do not bend as they are woven round.

1 Take eight sticks 25cm (10in) long, four of them from six foot butts and rather thicker than pencils. The rest are from the butts of thick five foots.

2 The four thick sticks must be trimmed before they will sit centrally in the block and will look neat at the finish. Do not make them too thin (Fig. 50).

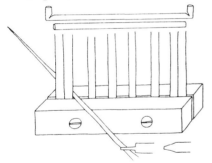

Fig 50 The square base:
sticks in the screw-block and the start of pairing.
Also showing the ways of cutting the sticks before putting
them into the block. Measuring aids shown above.

3 Stand these in the screw-block with 17cm (6¾in) between the outer edges. Space the other sticks between these, trimming them a little if necessary. Arrange neighbouring butts alternately up and down (Fig. 50).

4 *To start weaving*
Weave with three foots. Push the tip of one to the back between the left-hand pair and the next stake leaving enough at the back to travel the width of the base plus a little (Fig. 50).

5 Bring this tip round the two outside sticks and take it through on top of the other half and behind one stake and bring it back to the front (Fig. 51).

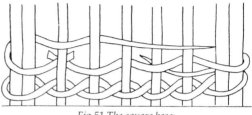

Fig 51 The square base:
the pairing and starting the randing

6 Use the two ends now at the front to pair to the end.

7 Take the tip round and weave it away.

8 Now take the butt end round the end sticks and continue weaving in and out. This is 'randing'.

9 Join another rod to the butt end crossing it at right angles. You can either join butts to butts and tips to tips, or join a butt to a tip. Always keep the joins on the back of the base as you work.

10 Continue to weave across, round the end posts and back, joining as necessary and keeping an even width.

11 This is fairly easy but note that the pulling around the posts tends to make the base get narrower. It is often hard to see this happening as it is so gradual but it is essential to have a measure and to *keep using it.* Either use a dry stick cut exactly to the length shown in Fig. 50 and keep using it just above the weaving or prepare a measure by cutting out two V-shaped notches in a stick and bending the ends round. Check by holding it above the weaving every few rows.

12 Every few inches rap the weaving down lightly. If you close it down too much it will be very hard to get the side stakes in.

13 Finish the base, when 23cm (9in) long, with a row of pairing. Start a new rod as you did at the beginning and pair with it, either threading through the butt at the end, this being the only end left on the front, or cram it off next to a stake.

14 Take the base out of the screw-block and pick it off. Cut off the ends of the sticks with shears.

Staking up

Before starting decide where you want the picked-off ends on the base to be. If the basket is to be for delicate things they should be left on the bottom but if it is to be on carpets they should be inside.

1 Slype on their backs the thirty-two thick three foots that are to be the stakes. Stake up the ends of the base with one stake per end stick (Fig. 52), and slyped surface uppermost. Put them into whichever side permits them to be spaced as evenly as possible. Use a bodkin and tallow as usual.

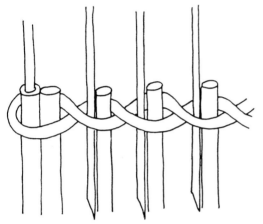

Fig 52 The square base: staking up the end

2 The outer ones are treated differently. A hole is made in the fat outside stick, pushing the bodkin well down into the pith (Fig. 52). The stake is then pushed into the centre of the stick. Prick all these end stakes up and put them in an oval hoop or tie them with string.

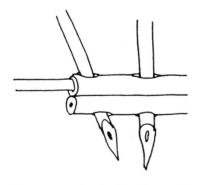

Fig 53 The square base showing the staking up of the sides:
(a) viewed from the top

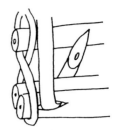

(b) seen from the side

(c)seen from the end,
without end stakes and outer row of base weaving

3 Side stakes

Be prepared to find this hard work at first. The side stakes are put in through the side sticks of the base between rows of weaving. They are spaced about 3cm (1⅛in) apart and it helps to mark their positions with pen or pencil on each side. Those at each end are put in about 1cm (¼in) from the end and the rest spaced evenly between them. Here there are eight on each side. Make sure the slypes are long and gently angled. The end stakes do not go in at right angles to the base sticks but along a line from the corner to the centre of the basket (Fig. 53a). Use a bodkin and push it into the side sticks from below at an angle of about 45° also pointing in away from the corner. Make a big hole, use tallow and then push in a stake. It will go through both base sticks and come to rest with the tip just resting on the first single base stick, or it should in an ideal world! Put in these four corner stakes first.

The rest go in from below at an angle of 45° but are at right angles to the edge of the base (Fig. 53a). Prick up all the side stakes about ⅛in away from the base and put them in the hoop.

Upsetting

1 Use four medium three foots. Bunch the tips. Place them as in Fig. 54a leaving about 8cm (3in) on the inside of the left-hand stake of

one end. Bring them to the front, take them in behind the next stake and bring them to the front (Fig. 54b). Leave them.

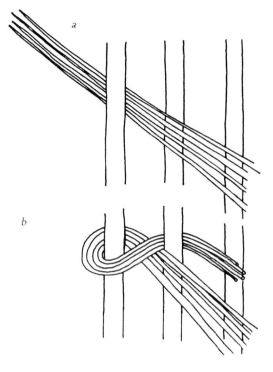

Fig 54 Starting the upsett:
(a) putting in the tips
(b) fixing them in position

2   Now leave one rod at the front, take one rod behind one stake and to the front, take another in front of one stake and behind one and to the front. The last passes in front of two stakes and behind one and to the front.

3   Now use these four rods for a four rod wale, tucking them well in between base sticks and stakes and pulling them tightly round the corners.

4   Start another set of four rods in the same way at the opposite end of the basket.

5   Then after working along two sides with each set drop one rod and continue with a three rod wale.

6   Join in three butts when necessary, preferably in the middle of an end or a side and certainly not on a corner. Work back to tips. As you move round the corners try to pull outwards the stakes on either side of each corner, they have a tendency to move in and it is not easy to pull them out later. Keep these stakes parallel to one another.

7   Take off the hoop.

Siding

This basket introduces a new stroke, 'English randing'. You will need weavers well matched in thickness. Sort them into short, medium and long and use the shortest first. Trim the tips of each group so all these rods are the same length. They do not need to be long enough to travel right round the basket.

1   Start the first weaver on the left of one of the long sides of your basket. The first long side you weave along will become the back of the basket.
Put a butt in to the right of the corner stake and resting against it. Rand this right round and out to its tip by going in front of one stake and behind the next (Fig. 55). Leave the tip on the outside. It should end before the butt is reached.

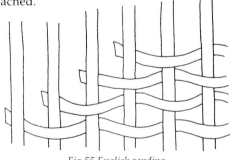

Fig 55 English randing

2   Put in another butt to the right of the first one. Rand with it until it runs out. The tip of this rod will overtake the tip of the first one, finishing one space to its right. Continue but do not put weavers in against the stake to the left of the two corner stakes, or the left-hand corner stake itself. The weaving will look uneven as you go up but this will correct itself when all the rods have been used. Continue until you have a complete round with one weaver in each space in the siding (minus those specified above).

3   Rap down the weaving lightly with the rapping iron or with the edge of the hand, as you go.

4   To control the shape

You may find that the basket is trying to become round as you weave up the side. The stakes tend to move towards the right and it is hard to keep the corners square. As you weave keep the two stakes either side of the corner as close together as possible and parallel to each other. You will need to keep pulling them outwards all the time to compensate for the weaving pulling them in. Adjust all the stakes as you weave by holding them where you want them.

If it looks as if your basket is going to flop out badly instead of going more or less straight up, it can be pulled in as follows. Take a slyped butt, push it in vertically beside a stake just above the upsetting or above some weaving on the far side of the basket, bend it down towards you across the basket, pull up the side towards you with it, take it between two stakes on the near side of the basket and weave it in and out for a few strokes. Several of these ties can be put in across the basket and one or two from end to end. When the basket is finished they are either pulled or cut out.

5   If this round does not give you the height you want go on randing until part of the basket reaches it. Next add in rods to build up the dropped part. This will mean using only occasional spaces but try to miss a regular number and arrange each weaver to alternate with the previous one to give the randed effect. Photos 17-19 show a basket with two complete rounds of English randing.

If one rod works as a slew for part of its length when building up, cut off its top inside the basket at the point where the slew would start. The next rod that comes round over it will give a rand.

The first complete rand may give the desired height to the siding but be of uneven height. Just weave an occasional rod on top to build up where necessary.

6   Top waling

Use a three rod wale. Lay in the three tips in three consecutive spaces on the left of one of the long sides. Work these out and join in three butts and work back to tips. Arrange to make the join in the centre of one of the sides.

7   Level off the basket.

Photo 18 Square basket showing the border square corners and the inside of the lid

Border (Photo 18)

This will be a four rod behind two border.

1   Select the best side of the basket as the front (here the side where the randing started) and start the border at the back.

2   Bend down the left hand stake taking it behind two stakes and out to the front. Bend down the next three to the right of the first, taking each in turn behind two stakes and out to the front.

3   Work until you have two stakes lying down between the two corner stakes (Fig. 56a).

Fig 56 The square corner as worked when the basket has blunt corners but the corner at the border is to be square. It is a four behind two plain rod border.
(a) on reaching the corner

4   Bring the next upright stake down into the corner as well, between the two that are already there (Fig. 56b).

54

*(b) bringing the stake down
to become the third one in the corner*

5 Gather up the three horizontal rods a, b, and c, by taking 'a' up to the corner stake, bringing 'b' beside it and then 'c' next door to that (Fig. 56c).

(c)gathering up the three stakes

6 These three are then used in reverse order. Take rod 'c' and lift it up into the air and kink it. The position of this kink should be in a straight line with the stakes of the second side of the basket.
HINT: It is this kink which forms the corner of the border so its position is very important.
Now fold this kinked rod 'c' over 'b' and 'a' and take it behind the second corner stake and bring it back to the front (Fig. 56d).
HINT: This stake never gains a partner.

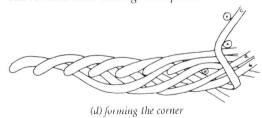

(d) forming the corner

7 Now 'b' is bent at a point just round the corner to start the straight line of the second side. Take it in front of one and behind the next upright stake and back to the front. Bring the first corner stake down beside it (Fig. 56e).

(e) using the second of the gathered up stakes

8 Now 'a' travels in front of two upright stakes and behind the next one and the second corner stake comes down beside it (Fig.56f).

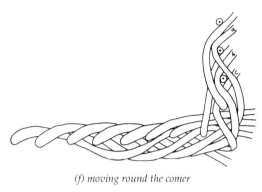

(f) moving round the corner

9 One of the three rods between the corner stakes is used next. Take the one touching the second corner stake. Pass it in front of two upright stakes, behind the next one and bring the next upright down beside it. The two rods remaining between the corner stakes are cut off (Fig. 56g).

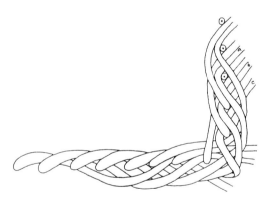

(g) starting to border down the second side

10 Now continue with the four rod behind two border using the solitary 'c' next and bringing a stake down with it. Work until you again have two rods coming between the two corner stakes. Go back to step 4 above and work the second corner in the same way as the first.

11 After the fourth corner finish the border as previously described for a four rod behind two border (p. 45). Pick off the basket.

The lid or cover
The size of this depends on the size of the top of the basket. If, being your first square basket,

it is very irregular why not put a cross handle on it? Make a lid for your next, better square basket. But if your first has fairly straight sides try a lid.

1 Setting it up

The screw-block is used again with stout butts from six foots for sticks. Only one is needed on each outer edge this time and because the lid will be wider than the base you will need an extra stick making seven. If you are having a handle you must have an odd number of sticks. Set them up in the screw-block, setting the outer ones the same width apart as that across the top of the basket minus 1cm (¼in) or so.

2 Start weaving with a row of pairing and then change to randing as with the base. If your basket is wider at one end than the other it is possible to make your lid to match by measuring carefully as you work and pushing the side sticks in or pulling them out as necessary.

3 Rand to the top of the cover sticks, rapping down at intervals, and finish with a row of pairing. The length of the lid should be about 1cm (¼in) short of the top basket length. The ends will be finished by bordering off with added stakes.

4 Cut off the inner cover stick ends but leave the outer ones on each end.

5 Pick off the lid.

6 Finishing the ends of the lid

(a) Extra stakes must be put in. Use fine three foot rods, slype them and push them into the weaving against the sticks except for the two on the right (Fig. 57a). Work with the picked ends on the lid towards you

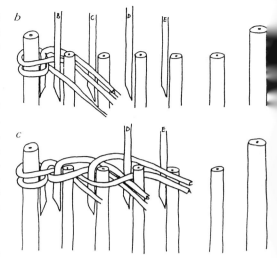

(b) Take another rod and loop it round the left-hand end stick and one of the upright rods with half on each side, then take the left-hand half right round again and back towards you (Fig. 57a and b). These two ends are used to start a two rod plain border.

(c) The left-hand end passes behind one stake and A is pricked down to sit beside it (Fig. 57b).

(d) The right-hand end is then taken in front of one and behind one and B brought down with it (Fig. 57c).

(e) A is used again and taken behind one and back to the front. C is brought down beside it.

(f) B goes behind one and D comes down with it. Now E is bent right round the end stick for one full turn and brought towards you again. Before this ring is pulled tight D is used again and crammed off beside the end stick where it will be held by the loop (Fig. 58).

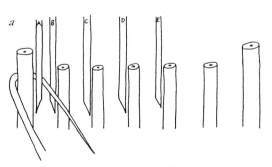

Fig 57 The edge of a square lid: starting

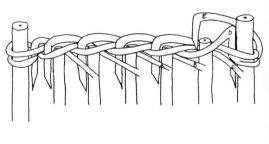

Fig 58 The edge of a square lid: finishing

(g) The end of E is now taken to the back of the lid, moving to the left, passed outside C and is crammed off to the left of the base stick which had no extra stake put in beside it.

(h) Repeat at the other end of the lid.
This is only one method of finishing the end of a lid. You will see variations if you examine square baskets with lids.

Single rod twisted handle
1 Find a fine perfect six foot or medium five foot. Slype it and, using a bodkin first, put it in beside the central stick about 8cm (3in) in from one end. Kink it by bringing it up vertically at its point of entry.

2 Twist it up. Carry it over in an arc, take it through the lid to the left of the same lid stick, loop it round this and thread it up on the other side. This makes the handle bow and should be about 8cm (3in) above the lid (Fig. 59a).

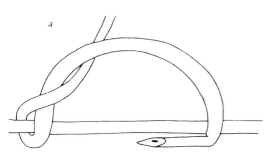

Fig 59 The single rod twisted handle
(the dotted part has just travelled)

3 Twist it up again if it has unravelled and wrap it round the bow until it reaches the other side. Pull as you wrap so that it distorts the bow and the two go together to look like two-ply wool (Fig. 59b).

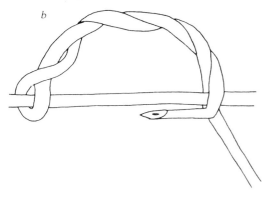

4 Take it to the other side, loop it round the stick and carry it back to the other side fitting it between the two twists already in position (Fig. 59c). Take it through the lid and weave it away to one side in between the randing. The effect should be of a three strand rope.

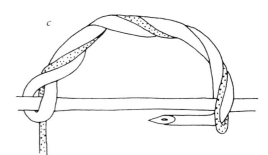

Hinges (Photo 19)
These are the simplest possible hinges but quite adequate on a small basket.

Photo 19 Back view of the square basket showing the hinges

1 Take a fine three foot rod and loop it round the third stake from one end of whichever long side is to be the back of the basket, taking it below the rows of waling (Fig. 60a).

2 Take one end in each hand and twist them round each other. Continue until about 6cm (2½in) is twisted.

Fig 60 Finishing the square lid:

(a) hinges

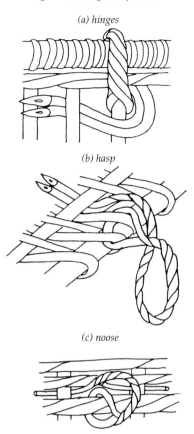

(b) hasp

(c) noose

(d) catch before pulling tight
(e) pulled hard and swinging on the noose

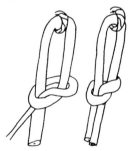

HINT: *This takes practice. Try to avoid one half of the rod spiralling round the other. Make each half move through 180°, one moving towards you and one away from you, with each twist.*

3 Arrange the lid in its best position and carry the twist over the edge stick of the lid, through between two rows of randing and back to the right of the original stake on the basket.

4 Carry both ends, untwisted now, to the left outside the hinge stake, behind the next and back to the outside where they are picked off against a stake.

5 Repeat to form the other hinge, making it as a mirror image.

Front fastening
On the lid
Take a fine three foot, thread it in the centre front of the lid round two or three rows of randing, and arrange half each side. Twist one half round the other again, form them into a loop about 2½cm (1in) long with the end crossing under the beginning (Fig. 60b). Thread the end under the first stick in from the edge. Weave them together in and out between two rows of randing, leaving them on the inside under the handle. This loop should be bent down towards the basket. This is the hasp.

On the basket
Use a long top from some other basket. Hook it like a hairpin round a row of top waling in the centre front. Twist the two ends and make a small loop about 1½cm (½in) diameter, taking the twist upwards and taking both ends to the inside (Fig. 60c). Take one end of the rod one way and one the other and weave them in and out for a few strokes under the border. You can twist up these ends to make the weaving away easier. This is the 'noose'.

Catch
Turn a thick four foot round a fat bodkin or thick pen about 15cm (6in) up from the butt. Thread the thinner side through the noose on the basket. About 5cm (2in) from the turn wrap it round the butt and thread the tip through its own loop and pull it tight in a knot. Cut off the two ends.
You could use a thick stick instead (Photo 17).

A SQUARE SHOPPER

An everyday basket, very useful for taking books back to the library (Photo 20).

Size
Height at handle 18½cm (7¼in), top 40cm (15¾in) by 29cm (11½in).(OM)

Materials
Either: 1½kg (3lb) five foots, a large handful three foots

or: about thirty-five five foots for stakes, fifty or so medium five foots for base weaving, waling and handle and a large handful of three foots for siding.

Photo 20 A square shopper with blunt corners

Eight stout butts of six foots for base sticks.
One handle bow, pencil thickness at the butt.
An oval hoop about 38cm (15in) long and 23cm (9in) wide.
Two thick handle liners.

The base

1   Arrange sticks from the eight butts of six foots in the screw-block with pairs on the outer edges, (butt and tip alternating), these being 20cm (8in) apart. The remaining four are evenly spaced between these two pairs.

2   Start with one row of pairing as before, using medium five foots.

3   Rand until the base is 30cm (11¾in) long, leaving all the ends on one side and keeping it a constant width.

4   Finish with another row of pairing.

Staking up

1   Slype thirty-one thick five foots on the backs.

2   Stake up one end of the base using six stakes and slyped surface upwards. The outer two go into the pith of the outer two sticks as before. Put each of the other four in beside a base stick. Prick these up.

3   Stake up the opposite end as before but this time use seven stakes, putting one on each side of one of the central base sticks. Prick them up. This provides an odd number of stakes and means you do not need to have two sets of slewing rods later on.

4   Put on the oval hoop and secure it with two stakes.

5   Put in nine stakes down each side of the base, making sure that one is central on each side. This makes provision for the handle. Prick them up ½cm (⅛in) away from the base, and put them in the hoop.

Upsetting

Two sets of four rods are used for this.

1   Start four tips of medium five foots on the left of one long side. Work these rods with a four rod wale round half the basket.

2   Start another set of four tips on the left of the second long side and work these down the side and across the end with a four rod wale.

3   Now one rod from each set is left behind and the two sets are used for a three rod wale. Work one set, joining in three butts when necessary, until they catch up with the other

set. Then use this second set and join when needed. Work both sets out to tips.

HINT: Arrange the butt to butt joins of both sets away from the corners and preferably in the centre of the long side.

4   Take off the hoop.

5   Put in handle liners on the left of the central stake on each side.

Siding: a three rod slew

This is a slight variation on the two rod slew. Because you have an odd number of stakes you will only need one set of weavers. Draft the material and use the shortest first.

1   Start with a single three foot with the butt on the left of one long side. Weave it in and out for about one-third of its length.

2   Add another rod, putting in the butt, and weave the two rods until two-thirds of the first rod is used.

3   Add a third butt so that you are slewing with three rods (Fig. 61).

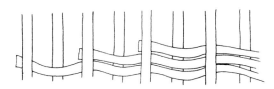

Fig 61 Starting a three rod slew:
each stroke is used to represent a third of a rod

4   Every time the bottom one runs out add in a new rod on top of the group of three.

5   Continue this slewing, taking care with the shape of the basket. Keep the two stakes next to each corner as close together as possible and parallel to each other. Pull them well out each time you go round them. The weaving will always tend to pull them in.
The sides will tend to flop outwards so keep them almost vertical. Use willow ties across if you need them. The side stakes will also need to be pulled away from the central stake to fill the space between this and the corner on each side. Keep all the end stakes out to get a flow. Rap down at intervals.

6   Slew until the basket is 12cm (4¾in) high at the centre side.

7 *Packing*

Here the sides of the basket are built up slightly.

Take a three foot, slype it and insert the tip (Fig. 62) and weave it as shown using randing. The gradual lengthening of the rows builds up the centre.

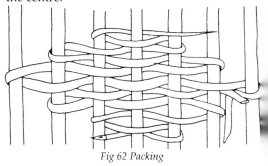

Fig 62 Packing

8   Put in another rod with a slyped butt and rand this as shown.

9   Repeat this packing on the opposite side of the basket.

10 *Top waling*

Start three tips of medium five foots on the left of each long side, carrying them over the packing. Work the sets to butts, making sure that when you catch up with the second set you start using them. Join both sets with three more rods and work them out to tips.

11   Rap down to make sure the two ends are the same height. Also rap down the sides to match.

The border: a four rod behind two border

This is a modification of the previous border giving blunt corners to go with the blunt corners of the basket.

1   Start with the stake next to the left-hand corner on one side. Bring down four stakes, kinking them 1cm (⅜in) above the siding, behind two stakes as before. Continue the four rod border until you have two stakes projecting between the two corner sticks on the right.

2 *To work the corner*

Bring the next upright stake down into the corner between the two already there. Keep all three side by side and pressed well down onto the top waling. Of these three only the middle one will travel any further (Fig. 63a).

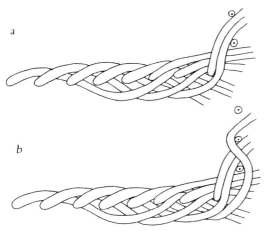

a

b

Fig 63 The blunt corner on a square basket: a four rod
behind two plain rod border

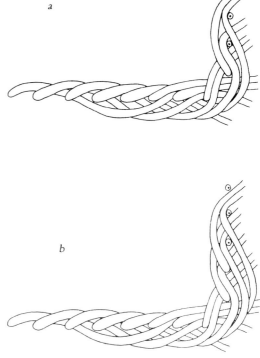

a

b

Fig 64 The blunt corner:
working the second side of the basket

3 Take the next horizontal stake you would use and pass it in front of the first corner stake, behind the second corner stake and back to the front (Fig. 63a).

4 The first corner stake comes down beside the rod you have just used (Fig. 63).

5 Take the left horizontal stake in front of the remaining corner stake, behind one upright stake and back to the front. Do not take this one round too tightly as this will tend to make it rise. This one remains single (Fig. 63b).

6 Take the right-hand horizontal rod of the remaining pair on the first side of the basket. Take it in front of two upright stakes and behind one and bring the second corner stake down beside it (Fig. 64a).

7 Take the middle of the three that are in the corner and put it in front of two upright stakes and behind the next one and bring an upright down beside it (Fig. 64b).

8 Then continue the four rod behind two border as before and work the corners as you reach them. Cram off to finish. Pick off the basket.

The handle

1 Take out the handle liners and put in a handle bow arranging it to be about 28 cm (11in) above base at its highest.

2 Rope it with medium five foots and finish off in one of the ways already described.

Where to go next

Having worked through the examples of willow-work given in this book try using what you have learnt to plan your own baskets. All the weaves described can be used for all shapes and sizes of baskets so try a few variations of your own. The techniques described are not the only ones that can be used. Many basketmakers have their own ways of doing things.

Discoveries of technique and design can be made by careful examination of baskets you may already have at home and of those in shops. Many gifts, such as soaps, are sold in small baskets and many of these, though often not well made, are very attractive. From these you may see new shapes, new ways of starting the waling, of finishing handles and so on.

If you are lucky enough to have professional basketmakers in your area examine their baskets too, and try to watch them being made.

Many museums, particularly museums of rural life, have fascinating examples of willowwork in the wide range of agricultural baskets used until relatively recently.

You might like to join the Basketmakers Association, a group of enthusiasts, both professional and amateur, who work to promote interest in the craft by publishing a newsletter and running courses. Further information can be obtained from Dr Maurice Bichard, The Farmhouse, Fyfield, Fyfield Wick, Abingdon, Oxon OX13 5NA.

Recommended reading

These few books will give you a lot of extra information. Unfortunately some are out of print but can probably be borrowed from your local library.

Elton Barratt, Olivia ed *Basketmaking* (London 1990)
A series of projects using many different materials and techniques, including willow work

Gabriel, Sue & Sally Goymer *The Complete Book of Basketry Techniques* (Newton Abbott, 1999)
A comprehensive guide to basketry, techniques and design, with an emphasis on willow work.

Heseltine, Alastair, *Baskets and Basketmaking* (Aylesbury, 1982).
This contains a brief history of English basketmaking and an excellent detailed description of the techniques used to make a general purpose farm basket with willow.

Knock, A G, *Willow Basket-Work* (Leicester, 1946)
This covers a wide range of techniques and a number of recipes for individual baskets. Very useful.

Maynard, Barbara, ed, Mary Butcher, *Modern Basketry Techniques* (London, 1989).
This deals with cane and willow, explains techniques clearly with illustrations and includes a large selection of recipes. Very good for beginners.

Okey, Thomas, *An Introduction to the Art of Basketmaking* (London, 1932 The Basketmakers' Association, 1994).
Detailed descriptions of techniques used in the making of a variety of functional and beautiful baskets. An excellent book by a master of the craft.

Wright, Dorothy, *The Complete Book of Baskets and Basketry* (Totnes, 1983).
A wealth of information about basketmaking in a wide variety of materials, their techniques and history. Also a stimulating collection of photographs.

Of interest too are the companion volumes to this book:

Bobart, H. H. (The Basketmakers' Association, Canterbury 1997) *Basketwork through the Ages*. A guide to the early history of basketmaking, originally published 1936.

Butcher, Mary, *Contemporary International Basketmaking* (Merrell Holberton, 1999)
Three essays, one historical, one on American Contemporary Work and one of Artist's Voices. Also a techniques section, resource list, and the Catalogue to the Crafts Council Touring Exhibition, 1999-2000.

Elton Barratt, Olivia, *Rushwork* (Dryad Press, London, 1986)

Johnson, Kay, *Canework* (Dryad Press, London, 1986).

Verdet - Fierz, Regula & Ternard *Willow Basketry* (Interweave Press, Colorado 1993)
Excellent detailed instructions of techniques with first rate illustrations, willow growing & harvesting information, tools etc.

Suppliers

CB Coate & Son	English Hurdle
Meare Green Court	Curload
Stoke St Gregory	Stoke St Gregory
Taunton	Taunton
Somerset TA3 6HY	Somerset TA3 6JD
Derham Bros.	Jacob, Young & Westbury
Fosters Farm	JYW. House
North Curry	Bridge Road
Taunton	Haywards Heath
Somerset TA3 6BB	Sussex RH16 1TZ

The first three suppliers listed grow their own willow and can supply buff, white or brown from three foot to eight foot long. The fourth supplier sells imported buff willows in most sizes.

Most of the baskets shown in this book have been made with willows from C B Hector & Son who have recently set up an English basket centre, now English Hurdle, and are experimenting with new varieties with various coloured barks. They can supply all sizes of steamed brown willow which is almost black, and an imported purple barked variety in three foot only. They have introduced 'starter' bolts which are mixed bundles of brown, buff and white in sizes up to and including five foots which are ideal for the beginner. They are also starting to pack smaller bundles by weight each approximately 5kg (10 1b).

Index